GOD

IS RIGHT
IN FRONT
OF YOU

Books by Brian Grogan, SJ

Daily Prayers for Jesuit Vocations
Dublin: Messenger Publications, 2012

Where To From Here? The Christian Vision of Life After Death
Dublin: Veritas, 2011 [US Edition: New York: New City Press, 2012]

To Grow in Love: A Spirituality of Ageing
Dublin: Messenger Publications, 2011

The Jesuits on Leeson Street 1910–2010 (editor)
Dublin: Messenger Publications, 2010

Meetings Matter! Spirituality & Skills for Meetings (with Phyllis Brady)
Dublin: Veritas, 2009

Alone and on Foot: Ignatius of Loyola
Dublin: Veritas, 2008

Our Graced Life Stories
Dublin: Messenger Publications, 2000

Finding God in All Things
Dublin: Messenger Publications, 1988

Finding God in a New Age
Dublin: Private printing, 1993

Love Beyond All Telling (with Una O'Connor)
Dublin: Messenger Publications, 1988

Reflective Living (with Una O'Connor)
Dublin: Messenger Publications, 1986

GOD
IS RIGHT
IN FRONT
OF YOU

A FIELD GUIDE TO
IGNATIAN SPIRITUALITY

BRIAN GROGAN, SJ

LOYOLAPRESS.
A JESUIT MINISTRY
Chicago

LOYOLA PRESS.
A JESUIT MINISTRY

3441 N. Ashland Avenue
Chicago, Illinois 60657
(800) 621-1008
www.loyolapress.com

First published in 1988 by Messenger Publications. 2nd Edition, 2014 by Messenger Publications.

Published in the United States of America in 2021 by Loyola Press.

Cover art credit: Copyright Artem Vorobiev/Moment/Getty Images, Colors Hunter—Chasseur de Couleurs/Moment/Getty Images, petekarici/E+/Getty Images, owngarden/Moment/Getty Images
Back cover author photo, Piaras Jackson, SJ.

ISBN: 978-0-8294-5022-4
Library of Congress Control Number: 2020949668

Printed in the United States of America.
20 21 22 23 24 25 26 27 28 29 Versa 10 9 8 7 6 5 4 3 2 1

Finding God . . . Falling in Love

"Nothing is more practical than finding God,
that is, than falling in love in an absolute, final way.
What you are in love with,
what seizes your imagination,
will affect everything.
It will decide what will get you out of bed in the
mornings,
what you will do with your evenings,
how you spend your weekends,
what you read,
who you know,
what breaks your heart,
and what amazes you with love and gratitude.
Fall in love, stay in love, and it will decide everything."

—attributed to Pedro Arrupe, SJ, Leader of the Jesuits 1965–1983

Contents

Foreword

There is, around the globe, a great interest in the spirituality of Ignatius of Loyola. If you have this book in your hands, you, too, have shown interest. Even if you already know about Ignatian spirituality, this book will put you in the hands of an author who knows what he is talking about. More importantly, you will meet a man with a big heart, a great love for God, and a knack for making Ignatian spirituality easy to grasp. He will introduce you to his master in the spiritual life, Ignatius of Loyola, the founder of the Society of Jesus, commonly called the Jesuits. But, like Ignatius, the author wants you to meet God and God's beloved Son, Jesus of Nazareth. I strongly urge you to read this book and to put into practice Brian Grogan's suggestions for knowing God better.

As the title of this book suggests, finding God is not as difficult as it sounds. True, God is Mystery itself and will always remain so. But, as Fr. Grogan explains, Ignatian spirituality takes seriously that God wants to be known by us. Indeed, God wants to be our friend. That's right—God wants to be your friend. In light of this truth, we can be confident that God will make himself known to us.

Ignatius of Loyola was, by his own account, a seemingly poor candidate for friendship with God when God visited him while he was recuperating from a critical battle wound. That visit from God came in a very ordinary way: through daydreams. Ignatius reasoned that if God revealed himself to him through his experience of daydreams and their aftermath, then God must be present everywhere and at every moment of our lives. In other words, Ignatius did not develop his way of helping people meet God through theory but through his own experience. But he had to pay attention to his experience and then figure out how God was communicating with him through that experience. This book will help you see that God is constantly trying to get your attention just as he ingeniously got Ignatius's attention when he was least expecting it. It will also help you discern how God is communicating to you through your experiences.

Ignatian spirituality is remarkably optimistic, possibly because Ignatius never stopped marveling that God would want his friendship. In addition, once he got his own bearings in this new life as a friend of God, he started telling other people about what he had learned and found that they, too, were transformed by meeting God personally. The result was that he wrote a book, *The Spiritual Exercises*, as a guide for those who wanted to help others meet God and be transformed. Like many how-to books, it's not always easy to read or understand.

Thank God for people like Brian Grogan, who have been transformed by making the Spiritual Exercises and who have a gift for writing. *God Is Right in Front of You* will help you meet God, who wants to be your friend. If you take Grogan's suggestions seriously, you will be transformed. Moreover, you will discover what you have yearned for your whole life, even if you did not know it. You, like all of us, want God, and God wants you. The amazing thing is that you don't have to work desperately at this. God is crazy in love with you (and all of us) and does all the heavy lifting himself.

—William A. Barry, SJ

Introduction

In 1996 I wrote a book titled *Finding God in All Things*. It was surprisingly popular, presumably because it spoke to many people whose lives are characterised by the quiet desire for God. That was eighteen years ago. Since then, many things have shifted, two of which are relevant to this revised edition.

Minor Mystics

Since Vatican II, the Church has been in the throes of change. A new Church is being born, however painfully. There are indeed many Christians who are unaware of what is happening, yet they are God-oriented folk who try to live good lives. They live by faith, put up more or less patiently with suffering, and hope that God will be revealed to them at the End. But there is also a growing body of Christians who are actively carrying the Church into the future. They are developing their personal appreciation of God. They are taking responsibility for their own growth and are using the riches that religion and spirituality offer to reach their full potential. They have a sense that the institutional and intellectual dimensions of religion are not enough for nourishment. They see that *the mystical dimension* is needed to sustain them in their God-given task.

Mysticism, the sceptics say, is five parts mist and five parts schism! Not so, said Karl Rahner, SJ, in a remark that has stood the test of time since his death in 1984. Rahner was a heavyweight theologian who discerned how things were moving after the Second Vatican Council, 1962–1965, and said that in the days ahead "a Christian will either be a mystic or nothing at all." This has brought mysticism into the spotlight. The theme of "finding God in all things" finds itself at home here.

By "mystic" he meant *someone who has experienced God for real.* The term *mystical* refers to seeing something hidden: it is an intuitional rather than an intellectual knowing of divine reality. Anyone, whether Christian or not, who tries to find God in daily life, will indeed find him and become a mystic at least on a minor level! God is not hard to find, as Paul of Tarsus reminded his skeptical Greek audience two thousand years ago. God is everywhere. It is in him that we live and move and have our being: God wraps us round closely, and nothing is outside the embrace of God (see Acts 17:28).

By taking your cues from a spirituality that helps you find God in everything, you will see God hidden under many disguises. Your searching and finding can go on forever. Life then becomes an exciting adventure, which carries great joy. Christian faith comes to life, and the Church grows. We are made, after all, for God, so in finding God we experience a rich depth of joy that does not fade. And since we reveal or hide God from one another by the depth of our appreciation of God, every finding of God can help others grow.

We can think of the Church as old and tired and "past it." Or we can take the longer view and contemplate how recently the Incarnation and the Church have emerged in human history. Perhaps the Christian community is only beginning to move toward adulthood. Rahner is sketching the next step we need to take to become truly mature Christians. For Pope Francis the Church of the future is to be a community of disciples, equal in dignity, who are sensitive to the presence of God in every aspect of their lives and who move together into the future through searching for God together.

Pointers to God

The difficulty in re-writing this book lies not in the fact that there is nothing new to say, but the opposite. When we talk about finding God *in all things*, immediately there is too much material to cope with because reality is quasi-limitless. And when we talk about *finding God*, we are talking about the Being who is Absolute Mystery and who is impossible to limit! My effort to revise the original pages of this book has been a challenging exercise of deciding what to refer to and what to leave you, the reader, to discover for yourself. All I can offer is a tiny map with arrows pointing in various directions and invite you to seek and find for yourself. I suggest that you ask God to reveal himself to you: Jesus *promises* that he will reveal himself to us (see John 14:21), and divine promises are the language of love.

We live within the Mystery that is God. God is not a mystery to be solved; rather, we are beings made for Mystery. God is totally beyond our grasp and always will be. But we are grasped by God, who sets us down in this world and sustains, invites, and welcomes us. Deep down in us is the desire for God. We are capable of knowing and loving God, whatever God may be. We too are holy mysteries: we cannot explain ourselves, and day by day we negotiate with others who also are mysteries.

God is God of the galaxies and the interstellar spaces. God is also involved in the tiny interactions that go on in nature and in human living. God is at home both in the micro- and the macro-levels of reality. God has a single loving plan which encompasses everything that exists or can exist. You can find God in nature, in the sky, in your own life, in prayer, in loving encounters, and even in sin and evil. So

I feel like the farmer in a Zen story: He looked up from his labours in the fields and saw the moon in its awesome splendour. Awestruck, he could do no more than point at the moon with a carrot. How many of his fellow farmers paid attention to him and looked up from their forced labour we do not know. But, following Rahner's hint, I invite you to put on your mystic glasses and search for God in the simplest details of life. There you will truly experience God for real!

Pope Francis

The invitation to find God in all things has moved center stage through the pontificate of Pope Francis, who was elected in March 2013. Francis is the first Jesuit pope, which means that he is a member of the Society of Jesus founded by St. Ignatius of Loyola and his friends in 1540. We will say more about Ignatius later; it suffices here to say that he wove into a spirituality his rich vision of God, of our world, and of our role in it. Ignatian spirituality offers to a vast number of people an attractive and exciting way of living the Christian faith.

The immense popularity of Pope Francis lies at least partly in his fostering of this spirituality. Everything Francis touches has the ring of God about it. The Church and even the world itself are beginning to catch on to what this means. Francis comes in "at ground level," as it were, and emphasises that God is to be met everywhere, in the beauty of human life but also in its messiness. God is not remote or institutionally bounded but instead dynamically alive and active in creation and human history. And this should not be a surprise, because what we refer to as "our world" is in fact God's, and God likes to work in it, improve it, and even play in it. Mostly God works with us rather than alone, and so we can at least sometimes find him. Gerard Manley Hopkins puts it well in *The Wreck of the Deutschland*: "I greet him the days I meet him, and bless when I understand."

Pope Francis's images of the Church are earthly: the field hospital, the mother, the tired and muddy traveller, and so forth. It is in the ebb and flow of earthly life that God is to be found. But God seems to delight in disguises, hiddenness, and silence. So, Francis is trying to point up some of the ways in which God may be found. In *The Joy of the Gospel*, 2013, he asks that the Church should face its many challenges by engaging in discernment. Christian discernment is an effort to seek and find God in decision making. It puts the divine agenda before any human agenda. We are to be led by God in all that we do. Principled disagreements around issues of Church practice and discipline must be tested against the Gospel. Thus opponents can explore issues from a common basis of belief and work together to see in which direction God may be beckoning. It was said of Ignatius that "he was led by Another." If an old Church is visibly dying, then the new Church which is slowly emerging will, if Pope Francis has his way, also be "led by Another." God is to be at the centre of the life of the People of God.

Gracious Mystery

From my own point of view, I too have shifted a little over the past eighteen years. I have been brought into a deeper appreciation of what "seeking and finding God in everything" may mean. From the perspective of ageing, the term takes on a new quality. Who or what will I meet when I meet God in death? I find that my sense of Mystery is growing. On all sides the "holy ground"—the territory of God—stretches out to the horizons. I am poorly equipped to encounter Pure Mystery, so to step into that domain which is God's alone can be a frightening prospect. And this remains true despite the divine invitation "Do not be afraid," which, according to Google, recurs sixty-seven times in the Bible! But there is also the conviction that the Mystery that beckons is gracious and befriending.

Pope Francis speaks of the *joy* of the Gospel. An aspect of that joy is to become more aware of the Divine Presence in each and every aspect of reality. We begin from a position of not-knowing. Slowly we awake, like Jacob, and find ourselves saying in wonder: "Surely the Lord is in this place, and I did not know it" (Genesis 28:16). In reality, God is in my world all the time, my world of joy and sorrow, of hope and fear, of birth and death, of beauty and horror. To be aware, however dimly, of the presence of God in this world changes everything. Imagine that the person you love is in a dark room: you can't see them but you know they're there. That is consoling.

The Mystery deepens as we go along and we see in some shadowy but real way. As the graduate said when asked how it felt to be at the end of studies: "It's been a great experience. I'm more confused than ever I was when I started, but on a higher level!" We get enough to encourage us to continue searching until we meet God directly. And even when we are bathed in God, there will always be more for us to savour. St. Paul tells us that love does not come to an end (1 Corinthians 13:8), and because God is Love Itself, there will be no end to our seeking and our enjoyment of him.

In the meantime, you are invited to ponder, reflect, and pray over what strikes you in these pages. May the various hints and intimations bring you many "moments of glad grace" and help you experience for yourself how God can be found everywhere. When you have caught on to this truth, you may find yourself perturbed when you hear someone remark at a debate, "Why bring God into this?" You feel like answering, "But you can't leave God out of it because God is in everything!" But you can learn to be patient with others, knowing that God is patient with you as you slowly discover the divine links attached to everything.

What's New Here?

In addition to the recasting of much of the original text, this revised edition contains extra chapters with new material. Each chapter remains short and can be read easily at a single sitting. At the end of each chapter you will find an exercise that will help you enter personally into some aspect of God's relationship with you.

Included as an Appendix is my pamphlet, *Finding God in a New Age*. Written in 1993 and now out of print, its inclusion here can serve as a resume of this book itself.

CHAPTER 1

How God Came in Search of Ignatius

Who Is Seeking Whom?

Seeking and finding God is not a new idea that began with Ignatius of Loyola. We find it over and over in scripture. The verse that comes most easily to us, perhaps, is from Jeremiah: "When you search for me, you will find me; if you seek me with all your heart, I will let you find me, says the Lord" (Jeremiah 29:13).

But who first searches for the other? Originally I titled this chapter "How Ignatius Came to Search for God," but I came to see—or was brought to see!—that I had the emphasis wrong: God first searches for us. God's first word to Adam is, "Adam, where are you?" (Genesis 3:9). The psalmist prays, "O Lord, you have searched me and known me . . . Search me and know my heart" (Psalm 139). The theme of God as "visiting his people" is strong in the history of revelation. It is fully achieved in the Incarnation. "He came to his own people" (John 1:11). In the resurrection appearances, Jesus is the one who takes the initiative in the encounters with his disciples.

And because we are creatures, seeking our Creator is a primary response of humankind and is the origin of the religious instinct.

"The wise person rises early to seek the Lord who made him" (Ecclesiasticus 39:5). Jesus says, "Search and you will find" (Matthew 7:7).

All Reality Seeks God

Searching for God is part of our DNA. St. Thomas Aquinas remarks that all created reality seeks God, by which he means that everything desires to continue in existence, and existence comes from God. Those wonderful people of 2,500 years ago who composed the scriptural Canticles had a deep sense of this. These songs ask all creation to "bless the Lord" (see Daniel 3:57–88, Psalm 148, and others). Sea monsters, mountains, trees, animals, heat, cold, and storm, kings and peoples, young and old—all have their role to play in the cosmic choir as it praises God. In this sense all created reality participates in seeking and finding God. When we are struggling alone to find God, it is encouraging to know that we are being carried along by this cosmic dynamic. Our need for God is not accidental to us but expresses our total reality. It can rightly be said that each of us *is* a cry for help, each of us *is* a need for God.

But back to Ignatius, who witnessed in his own story and his teaching how we can be helped to find God in a personal way.

What Was Ignatius Like?

Ignatius of Loyola, 1491–1556, was, first and foremost, a real person; he was enthusiastic, alive, warm, and attractive, a visionary leader, capable and energetic. As his life moved on, he slowly became more reflective about what was going on in himself. He became a man passionately in love with God and the world around him. He came to understand that this world, which we think of as *ours*, is in fact God's world and that God is busy in it and can be found everywhere in it.

Historically Ignatius spans two worlds. He was born in an obscure place, Loyola (the name means "a bog"), in the Basque country of

Northern Spain at the end of the Medieval Period. But he lived out his life in the world of the Renaissance. He was small, liked to dress well, and as yet did not carry the limp that resulted from a battle in 1521. As a young man he was shaped by the medieval traditions of knighthood and chivalry. Had God not dramatically intervened to beckon him in a different direction, he might have lived out the life of a conquistador and died violently and unremembered.

Conquistadors

The Spanish word *conquistadores* means "conquerors." They played an important role in the Spanish and Portuguese colonisations of Central and South America in the sixteenth century. They were knights, individualistic, completely themselves. There was nothing of the "unknown soldier" about them. They had a passion for personal reputation and were full of prickly pride. They disliked discipline and regimentation and insisted on being consulted about every decision. On the other hand, they were totally committed to their chosen lord. This helps to explain their extravagant daring and their indifference to wounds, fatigue, and even death. They conducted themselves with the high seriousness of men conscious of taking part in great deeds.

Ignatius pulsed with the blood of the conquistadors. No wonder, then, that he was willing in 1521 to defend Pamplona, single-handed if necessary, for the sake of his lord, the Duke of Najera. The same year saw the fall of Mexico City to Cortes. Cortes had only a tiny army, but it kept together in spite of incredible hardships because of the personal bond between soldier and leader. Out of this period, then, Ignatius emerges as dreaming impossible dreams, single-minded and totally committed, with a conviction of his own importance in the scheme of things and of the rightness of what he was doing.

Enter God

During the siege of Pamplona, Ignatius's leg was badly injured by a cannonball. He was then about thirty years old. He lay in bed for a long time and suffered much while it healed. He liked to read and dream of adventure, but, unfortunately, there were no interesting novels or adventure stories to hand; the only books available to him during this time were the *Life of Christ* and the *Lives of the Saints*.

Reading these stories, he slowly began to dream a different dream. He pondered on the purpose of life and found, to his surprise, that his allegiance was shifting from an earthly to a heavenly lord. In his own words: "I was like a man roused from heavy slumber . . . What strange life is this that I am now beginning to live?" Those around him said that he became "a new man with a new mind." How did this happen?

Jesus Becomes His Lord

From reading the *Life of Christ* and the *Lives of the Saints* Ignatius came to see—with a shock—that God loved him and was personally interested in him. Being imaginative, Ignatius was able to enter fully into the scenes of the Gospels. He now saw Jesus as the true Lord, the one whose enterprise was truly worthwhile, the one who had suffered and died and risen for him. He became aware that God was *for him*, on his side, and had always been so. Overwhelmed, his initial response was one of gratitude. Why was God so good? But there was no answer. *There is no answer.* God is just like that.

It is consoling for us that thirty years of his life had passed before Ignatius began to engage in the mysterious encounters the human heart can have with God. Such encounters are intensely private and unwitnessed—and usually unrecorded. Yet we too can have these encounters because God meets us in every situation.

When Ignatius caught on to what was happening, he began to record his experiences. In his meetings with others he found it helpful to share something of how God was dealing with himself and how he dealt with God. But each life is unique, and Ignatius's gift lay primarily in his ability to enable others to enter a process of contemplative reflection whereby they could meet God directly themselves and come to understand how God was engaging with them in their own life situations. Recall the images of the sculptor and the dancing tutor!

Thus was born his little book called *Spiritual Exercises*. The exercises became immensely popular and are today more so than ever. This is because we all have to make decisions, and we want to make them well and find God in them. We will return to this topic later.

Change of Direction

As a result of what he had experienced, Ignatius changed his lifestyle. The knight became the pilgrim, which is the title he gives himself in his *Autobiography*. He lived as a beggar and a hermit and tried to emulate the saints in a crude and untutored way. He had great desires to serve God, but he had much to learn about how God wished to be served. Fully eighteen years went by before he saw that God was calling him to found a religious order. This order was to be a group of like-minded men fired with the desire of being totally at the service of God and humankind within the Church.

The last sixteen years of his life (1540–1556) were spent in a small room in Rome, administering the affairs of the newly born Company of Jesus or "Jesuits," which he and his companions had founded. He had moved from knight to pilgrim to founder and finally to administrator. Like many of us, he found that life evolves in very unexpected ways.

We know from Ignatius that he had one simple goal after his conversion. It was "to help others." He found administration irksome. He would have preferred to be engaged in direct pastoral work and to give others his beloved *Exercises*. But we also know that he had learned to allow God to take the initiative in shaping his life. In his *Autobiography*, dictated in the third person shortly before he died, we read in the literal translation:

> . . . Always growing in devotion, i.e. in facility in finding God, and now more than ever in his whole life. And every time and hour he wanted to find God, he found him.
> (Munitiz, J & P Endean: *Saint Ignatius of Loyola: Personal Writings*. London: Penguin, 2004, 63). Hereafter referred to as *Ignatius: Writings*.

In whatever situation, dramatic or dull, finding God was for Ignatius the key issue, and so it provides the limitless dynamic of his spirituality.

Transformations

It may help to summarise the transformations that went on in Ignatius's way of seeing things by which he steadily grew in his capacity to find God.

Thus the younger Ignatius is obsessed with desire for worldly honours and glory. But the mature Ignatius lives only for the honour and glory of God and finds himself directed to the poor and marginalised.

And, where before his conversion he is ready to kill if honour requires it, later he wants only "to help others" in any way he can. He will no longer use arms to sort out problems between people but rather the gifts of reverence, listening, helpful teaching, encouragement. Intractable situations he respectfully leaves to God.

In the early stages of his conversion, he tries to storm heaven by self-imposed penances and by deciding to reside in the Holy Land. Later he learns not to run ahead of God or to spoil God's work of art but to recognise that every place is holy ground because God is already there. Instead of making decisions to please himself, Ignatius allows his life to be taken over by Another and he becomes a person who wants only to be open to what might please God. Instead of guessing what might in fact please God, he learns the art of discernment and the signs of God's approval.

Although his heart becomes, in his own words, "ablaze with God," he has to learn to shift from trying to do great things for God by individual effort to labouring with God and in companionship. Next, the private love affairs of his pre-conversion years yield to a love affair with God and to a transparent love for everyone. He learns that all human loves are good when set within the embrace of divine love. His interest shifts from the petty wrangling of local lords to the universal concern of the "Eternal Lord of all things, the Divine Majesty."

One could go on and on highlighting the changes that characterised Ignatius's inner pilgrimage from his own small self-centred world to the limitless world whose Centre is God. But the message for us is to allow God to lead us through whatever transformations God may have in mind for us. It is not for us to set boundaries on God's work. Our tiny planet, wending its way among the stars, needs people who love it and its precious inhabitants with a love that "comes from above," as Ignatius liked to say.

SUGGESTED EXERCISE

- Find a place that can be yours for a little while; perhaps sit in a friendly chair, or in a corner that you have designated as a sacred space, or in the garden.

- Generally speaking, it is good to fix the same time each day to meet the Lord. Initially it may be difficult to organise, but after a while it is surprising how you will find yourself looking forward to it. The anticipated meeting becomes precious.

- Make yourself comfortable; if you are indoors, you might light a candle. Trust that God is there with you and that he has been prompting your heart to talk to Jesus.

- Enter the delightful scene from the springtime of Jesus' ministry (John 1:35–39). You are standing near the Lake of Galilee with John the Baptist. You see a figure in the distance and hear John say to you: "Look, there is the one who takes away the sin of the world!"

- You look at Jesus for the first time. You experience his attractiveness, and you begin to walk towards him. He turns around and looks at you. What is that look like?

- You hear him gently ask, "What are you looking for?" What is his voice like? Has anyone ever spoken to you before in such a welcoming and sensitive tone?

- Respond as you can. Let the conversation take off from there.

CHAPTER 2

Finding God in Our Experiences

The following pages offer a simple introduction to Ignatian spirituality, not a scholarly analysis demanding great effort and concentration on your part. But I am inviting you to get involved in something that can well change your life—for the better! I am inviting you into the kitchen rather than into the library. Ignatian spirituality is participative, not a spectator sport! The ideas outlined here have value only insofar as they evoke an experience for you or make sense of the vast array of experiences that make up your personal history. They are intended to open windows into the relationship between God and yourself. My hope is that you will gradually become a living witness to the truth that God can be sought and found in all things.

What Is Spirituality?

The word "spirituality" can be a real stumbling block! One of my colleagues wrote a tome analysing some thirty-eight variant meanings for it. I suggest simply that you think of it in terms of a relationship. So a spirituality of marriage answers the question, "What has marriage to do with my relationship with God?" Likewise a spirituality of suffering tries to indicate how we can grow in our relationship with God in times of suffering and pain. A spirituality is asserting that God can be found in the area of experience being dealt with. Our experiences, no matter how humble, messy, or even shameful, are the raw material in which we find God.

What differentiates spirituality from theology is its focus on the actual, living relationship between us and God in real-life situations. This relationship is meant to be one of ever-growing awareness of God's presence and involvement with us in the present and the concrete. This awareness can eventually cover the whole of life, if we work at it. In his *Autobiography*, written towards the close of his life, Ignatius could say that "his devotion, that is, his ease in finding God, was always increasing, now more than ever in his entire life. *At whatever time or hour he wanted to find God, he found him*" (99). Hence a handy summary of Ignatian spirituality is "Finding God in all things."

Family Prayer?

While the phrase "finding God in all things" points to a transcendent vision, it can be daunting. Some people may never have even thought of finding God in anything. They might say, "Finding God in *something* for a start appears possible, but finding God *in all things* is a bridge too far!" Ignatius would always accept people where they found themselves. He would invite them to take a little step forward and to move along at their own pace. After all, Ignatius would admit, God worked at Ignatius's own slow pace. He tells us that God dealt with him as a schoolmaster with a dull pupil! God knew what would attract his attention. God played on his burning desire to become distinguished by great deeds and led him on until he surrendered to God's dreams and became able to find God in everything.

Grace comes tailor-made to each of us, and the trick is to know what will help us find God at any given time. One of my cousins felt challenged through a homily to bring prayer into the family home. He discussed the matter with his wife, and they agreed that the Family Rosary was the thing to do. The five children knelt down on cue after dinner and the father led off. There were some giggling and shuffling. Then Lucy, one of the family members, got up and went around peering into each person's face in turn and finally went back to the fireside and howled. This was the end of the Rosary as family prayer in that household. Lucy, by the way, was a golden Labrador.

I showed up some weeks later with everyone bursting to tell the story. Then we got chatting about a new approach. Could they start with themselves? Could they imagine that each of them, as they sat around the family table, was the image of God, but disguised? Could they believe that the love that usually prevailed among them was a hint of what God is like? Could they agree that when they were awkward or irritable, their disguise was very good? We made a game of this, and I threw in a word for Lucy, who was always so good-humoured even when she was ignored for hours on end. Lucy, they agreed, reflected something of God in her own canine way. Bit by bit, progress was made, and finding God in everyday things became part of the style of the family.

Contemplative in Action

It can help as we go along to have in mind another summary statement of Ignatian spirituality. One of Ignatius's early companions used the term "Contemplative in Action" to try to capture Ignatius's way of being present to life around him. So let us unfold it a little because it can serve to describe ourselves to some degree.

Contemplation is usually thought of as spending long periods of undisturbed time focussed on God. If I think of it only in that way, then I will presume that God likes me more when I am praying than when I am working or enjoying myself. Prior to Ignatius's day the contemplative life, usually lived out in a monastery or convent, was considered superior to the active life. The active life was thought of as only an *indirect* mode of relating with God. Ultimately, the argument went, we are destined for the beatific vision of God, so we should be practising it as much as we can here below. The little drama in Bethany was used to illustrate the point (Luke 10:38–42). Jesus has shown up: Martha goes into overdrive; she is distracted with getting a nice meal ready for their special visitor. Mary sits at the feet of Jesus, watching, listening to him. Jesus affirms that Mary has chosen the better part. So in the history of the Church, Mary became the model of the contemplative life, and it took precedence over the active life exemplified by Martha. And yet we are left with a niggle: surely humdrum work has a real value in God's eyes? After all, God worked for the six days of creation before resting! Surely God is a working God who enjoys getting things done?

To Please God in Everything

The genius of Ignatius was to weld into one the active and the contemplative. For him, the important thing is *always to do what God wants*. If God calls me to pray or contemplate, I do that. If God calls me into active service, I do that. Either way, I am to be fully available and open to God. I learn by discernment the balance between prayer and activity. What became known as apostolic prayer, the prayer of an active disciple, is characterised by asking God what I am to do. I reflect on the options and on my past experience. I chat with God, asking, in Ignatius's words, "What ought I do for you?" I return to work with renewed vision and energy. Love for God orients me, and I find God as I go. I meet God "in the field."

Of course I could get lost in endless activity without surrounding it with contemplation. Often I "do my thing" without asking God what he wants done. But when we learn to be contemplative in our activity, we are indeed at the wheel, but God is navigating. We try to be attentive to divine guidance. Our desire is to please God. We live in familiarity with God—another Ignatian term—and we develop a lively interior life, where no compartmentalising occurs because we are centred on God. We are at home with God whether active or praying. We trust the world as a place where God dwells and labours. This is why it is said that Ignatian mysticism is *a mysticism of service*. It is a finding of God in the middle of activity.

To be contemplative even in action is a stance, a dynamic way of proceeding. We are watching out for sightings of God all around us, and we try to find the divine life at the heart of reality. Ignatius left no detailed rule about how much prayer his followers should undertake. Instead he asked that we should *keep God always before our eyes*. This is contemplation in action. It is a tall order, but we know what it is like to be doing something, whether pleasant or distasteful, with someone else in our mind. I came across migrants working in the diamond mines of South Africa. They endured long hours in the depth of the earth in order to send money home to their families.

Contemplation has been described as "a long, loving look at the real." This is how God looks at our world. Then God "gets going" and intervenes on our behalf. In this sense, God is THE "contemplative in action." So, of course, is Jesus. He prays, he works, he suffers, but always in the presence of his Father. He has a discerning heart, which is why he can say "I always do what is pleasing to him" (John 8:29). As his companions, we try to imitate him. It is no accident that the first Jesuits wanted to be known as "companions of Jesus."

SUGGESTED EXERCISE

- Scripture references are offered here to help you know that the suggestions are based in the word of God.
- Find a suitable time and a comfortable place where you can have quiet time.
- Invite Jesus to the home of your heart, just as Mary and Martha used to do (see Luke 10:38–43).
- How do you prepare your "secret place" for his coming? (See Matthew 6:6)
- Do you open the door as he nears the house or wait for him to knock? (See Revelation 3:20)
- How does he look at you? And how does his gaze affect you? (Mark 10:31)
- When the welcomes are over, you sit together and chat. You share with him whatever you wish—you can tell him about your day, your problems, your hopes. (See Mark 6:30)
- How does he listen? What does he say? (See John 14)
- How does your meeting end? A kiss, a hug, a promise to get together again soon . . .? (See John 14:28)

CHAPTER 3

Seeing Myself as God Sees Me

Some time ago I was asked to talk to a group of seminarians on how I pray. "They know the theory," I was told, "but they'd like to hear how other people in fact go about it. There are plenty of good books on how to pray, but what would help would be an honest outline of *how you actually pray!*"

I was not asked to speak about the daily Eucharist and the Ignatian Review of Consciousness, nor of moments of quiet adoration in an empty chapel. Such interludes were considered to look after themselves, as it were. The seminarians felt that they were "at home" at such points. I mentioned in passing that "adoration" comes from the Latin and infers "putting your hand to your mouth and saying nothing." This was intriguing and helpful.

This was for me a new challenge. It might be so for you too. Think about it in a spare moment. It took me a while to begin to notice what I do in the time of prayer and—which is more important—what happens to me in the doing. I should say here that I have been a Jesuit for the past sixty years, and so I have long been in an environment of prayer, which is a great support. Religious life without prayer is strictly meaningless, when we understand prayer as an expression of the relationship between God and ourselves.

So before moving into an analysis of what finding God in *all things* is about, I will describe what *finding God in prayer* looks like for me. I shall divide what follows into two parts:

- "Quality prayer time" when the only item on the agenda is prayer (chapters 2 and 3).
- Informal prayer, by which I mean the relating with God that can go on through the day when, like Martha of Bethany, I am busy about many things (chapter 4).

Quality Prayer Time

Let's start at the very beginning of the waking day! While I am summoning up the willpower to get out of bed, I find myself running through various simple prayers—old favourites, such as Hopkins' poem "*Thee God I come from, to thee go . . .*" or his "*O God I love thee . . .*" This habit, of course, can serve as a delaying tactic against the task of getting up! I have the intention of spending an uninterrupted hour with God each day: this includes praying parts of the Divine Office, but erosion can occur at either end of the hour! I can leave God waiting or terminate our engagement abruptly.

I get out of bed earlier than I would wish: I would love another hour between the sheets. So I get up when I do, simply in order to pray. I do this because I need regular time with God, just as a plant needs regular watering and friends need quality time together. If I didn't have a relationship with God, I'd stay in bed longer—and sometimes in fact I do just that, which usually means that I miss out on formal prayer time for the day. I have gone through over-busy periods when my prayer was no more than a mumbled "Good morning, Lord, bless the day!" I have no doubt that my God is an understanding and sympathetic God and accepts the briefest of acknowledgements. But these were not the best times in my life. To miss out on quality-time prayer is for me to miss out on something important. Perhaps nothing seems to be going on: "I don't get much out of it" is my usual phrase. But all I can say is that there is a better atmosphere about the days when I pray than about those when I don't.

I like the advice of Thomas Blake, a 17th-century author:

Every morning lean your arms awhile upon the window-sill of heaven, and gaze upon your Lord. Then, with that vision in your heart, turn strong to meet the day.

And I also like Rabindranath Tagore's prayer:

I have come to thee to take thy touch before I begin my day
Let thy eyes rest upon my eyes for awhile.
Let me take to my work the assurance of thy comradeship, my
friend.
Fill my mind with thy music to the last through the desert
of noise.
Let thy Love's sunshine kiss the peaks of my thoughts,
and linger in my life's valley where the harvest ripens.

—From Rabindranath Tagore: *Lover's Gift and Crossing*
NY: MacMillan, 1918

I usually light a candle: It will be there, burning steadily, even if I am all over the place! I sit at my window because I like to be rooted in the real world—currently I have the rear of a hospital as my view. I have come to like that. It mirrors my own need for healing, for tender care. I am like the patients whom I can see there: I too present myself daily for treatment.

God's Gaze

St. Ignatius was a wise old bird in the matter of relating with God. "Don't rush into it," he would say. "Instead, first consider how God is looking at you." The Spanish word is *mirar*, which connotes a steady gaze, and it is a gaze of love, a contemplative gaze. Ignatius uses it to describe how the three divine Persons look at the world in all its pain and tragedy and then work out their plan for our salvation. The word "admire" is drawn from the word *mirar*, "to gaze." Could it be that God actually *admires* me? After all, am I not his handiwork . . .?

St. Teresa of Avila uses the same word *mirar* and advises the same practice when we enter contemplation of the Lord in the Gospels: "Gaze on him who gazes on you, and how he looks on you, lovingly and humbly." Here we have mutual contemplation—that "long, loving look at the real." Firstly it is God who contemplates us, and in return we contemplate God. This is an utterly simple practice, but it is also a profound way of praying.

I used to spend time in a heady way reflecting on how God might see me on any given day. I used to think, "God must love me when I attend to him and must be irritated when I ignore him." Of course, this got me nowhere. I was simply spinning out my subjective images of God. Then, by some grace, I came to see that I have no right to presume that I can see into the mind of another, especially if that other is God. I must let God speak directly to me.

From Wondering to Asking

So instead of simply thinking my all-too-human thoughts, I addressed God: "Well, how do you see me today?" And I noticed that I kept on getting drawn back to the line, "I have loved you with an everlasting love; therefore I have continued my faithfulness to you" (Jeremiah 31:3). This, I accepted, was God speaking directly to me, and it changed everything. Now I was sure of God. And I was listening, not to myself and my moods of confidence or uncertainty but to the unqualified Good News. First and foremost for me now is the truth that I am "the beloved of God" (Romans 1:7).

Since then, I mostly start my prayer-time by asking God, "How do you see me?" I linger over the unwavering response expressed in varying ways in Scripture: "You are my beloved, my work of art, my image, my likeness, my friend." The same comforting message recurs: "You are OK, because I love you!"

To be gazed on with love is the very making of a human being. Worlds open up for infants who receive the loving gaze of their mother. Loving looks are relational and can be transforming. At a family wedding recently, the groom spoke of his first encounter with the woman who was to become his wife. "She was beautiful," he said, "and was gazing in my direction. I turned to see the lucky person behind me, but there was no one there. I looked at her again, and her face opened into the perfect smile. She was looking at me! I was stuck to the bar stool, but she came over and said, 'Hello.' That's where it all began!"

We can imagine the unwavering gaze of Jesus on his disciples, from the time he first met them to the moment when he sat down to his Last Supper with them. It was surely the glance of pure love. Then there is the rich young man of whom it is said, "Jesus, looking at him, loved him" (Mark 10:21).

A 17th-century French mystic summed up the relationship between herself and God: "You gazed on me and you smiled!" That is enough. God's gaze is a gaze of blessing. That gaze roves over the world, while we are busy about our affairs and also while we sleep. God blesses us all, all the time. I can learn to gaze as God does, and to bless all humankind. This brings a softness to my relationships when I meet with people who are just that bit difficult!

"A Very Good Place to Start"

Behind all of this stands the primordial statement: "God saw everything that he had made, and indeed, it was very good" (Genesis 1:31).

A contemporary translation runs: "It was so good, so very good!" We are created and sustained by the loving and affirming gaze of God. There is no better place for me to start my prayer than here.

Sometimes, in fact, this is the only steadily discernible form I can find in my prayer. It comes at the beginning and can endure quite a while. Sometimes there goes on a silent communication, when I am drawn into the welcoming Mystery. Sometimes, however, the middle of my prayer time is a shapeless muddle. The end, too, can be a disjointed fade-out rather than a respectable conclusion. I often just stop praying, stand up, and get myself ready to face the day without an "Adieu."

But the start is rich. It is the gift that keeps me going for the day. The truth that I am the beloved of God changes everything. It is both comfort and challenge. I can depend on it more than on anything else in the world. I want to live up to it, but even if I don't, I will be reminded next day that I am still unconditionally loved, no matter how mediocre I have been. Also, loving others becomes a bit easier when I become aware of their deepest truth: no matter how disguised, each of them also is a "beloved of God."

SUGGESTED EXERCISE

- Find your favourite place, settle down, and prepare to meet Jesus.

- When he comes, notice how alive he is, how interested in everything, as if he sees things with fresh eyes rather than with a bored glance.

- Now notice those eyes set on you. What is it like to be the focus of his undivided attention? Do you feel happiness, or are you embarrassed or troubled?

- Recall other people who have gazed on you with undisguised love.

- Now stand with him at a window, facing the street where people are passing.

- He asks me, with deep feeling, "Do you think these people know who they really are? Each is a masterpiece; each is a daughter or son of God. Each is the image and likeness of God. They're all extraordinary immortals. They each carry the mystery of their divinity. Isn't it wonderful? But do they know all this?"

- I reply, "I doubt it . . . But I'm just like them: I don't think about myself that way at all. I feel I miss so much by just taking myself for granted as ordinary, unremarkable . . ."

- He puts his arm around me and whispers, "Perhaps from today on you might start seeing yourself and others this way. Will you try it? It changes things!'"

- "Yes, I will," I say. "But keep reminding me . . ."

- Stay with him as time allows. Then say good-bye to him and plan to meet again.

CHAPTER 4

Chatting with God: You and I, Lord

Let us move on from glance to words. The interpersonal quality in the loving glance of God brings into focus the fact that we do well to address God directly, because God addresses us so. I can spend too much time reflecting *about* God—third-person-singular stuff, such as "I wonder what God thinks of what I've done now?" "Does God care about the mess I'm in, or how I feel?" "Perhaps God is angry with me?" "I'm mad with God right now!" And so forth.

But when I switch to talking directly to God, everything changes. "What do you think of what I've done now?" "Do you care about the mess I'm in, or how I feel?" "Are you angry with me?" "I'm mad with you right now!" "Lord, I'm too tired to pray, please excuse me, bless me and give me a good night's rest." Now I am in dialogue and I am bringing God in on what is happening, rather than keeping him at a safe distance.

So I enter into the world of the Jews whose chatting with God fills the Hebrew Scriptures. God addresses Adam and Eve directly, and they tell their sad tale in return. Abraham bargains with God to save the people of Sodom and Gomorrah. Moses and God speak together as friends. The psalmist dialogues with God about all his concerns and takes it for granted that he will be taken seriously. He gets worked up, lets God know how he is feeling, and offers plenty of uncalled-for

23

advice on what to do with the wicked. It is stern and robust stuff, but it is healthy and helps to clear the air! The Prophets tell God what they think: "You have overpowered me, and you have prevailed" (Jeremiah 20:7).

When we come to the New Testament, the dialogue between God and ourselves is obvious throughout, through the person of Jesus as he engages with the disciples. We are also shown that Jesus relates directly with his Father; his prayer is an intimate dialogue: "Father, if you are willing, let this cup pass from me" (Luke 22:42). Clearly, God seems to see chatting as a right way to relate!

Martin Buber, a Jewish author, thought the interpersonal connection created between persons by using first- and second-person singular so important that in 1923 he wrote a book titled "*I and Thou.*" The book was an effort to counter our tendency to see everything as objects: the material world, people, and even God. Thus we distort and impoverish reality, we abuse our environment and our neighbour. And we get locked into an infantile relationship with our God. While it is challenging to treat the material world reverently as a "thou," we must learn to do so for its very survival—and our own. Further, each of our fellow humans is to be treated as a "thou"—we must never say of another, "That person means nothing to me." Finally, if we are to be in real relationship with the divine, we must relate to God as "Thou."

The Don Camillo series by Giovannino Guareschi reveals humorously and attractively the power of a strong interactive relationship with God. Don Camillo is an Italian pastor in a small post-war town that has all sorts of problems, including the Communist mayor, Peppone. The good pastor chats everything out with Jesus, who is hanging on the great crucifix in the church. The interactions are full of the stuff of real life. Jesus gives as good as he gets, and Don Camillo is constantly invited to a broader and more inclusive view of things.

As One Friend to Another

The scriptural understanding of prayer as conversing with God is carried forward in Christian spirituality, though it tends to get obscured by formal and vocal prayer, where we use the words of others rather than our own. St. Teresa of Avila articulates a long tradition when she says, "Mental prayer is nothing else than an intimate friendship, a frequent heart-to-heart conversation with God by whom we know ourselves to be loved."

Ignatius had the same idea in proposing the "colloquy" as a way of praying. "Colloquy" means "speaking together." It involves a personal and spontaneous conversation, a chat, between friends. Ignatius says,

> Imagine Christ our Lord present before you and nailed to the Cross, make a colloquy ... A colloquy means speaking as one friend speaks with another, at times asking for some favour, at other times accusing oneself for something badly done, or sharing personal concerns and asking for advice about them.
>
> (*Ignatius: Writings*, 296)

Elsewhere Ignatius praises what he dares to call "familiarity with God." We need to dare to engage in this familiarity. For a friendship to deepen, persons need time alone with each other: time to talk and time to listen; time to explore one another's lives and to catch on to their different values, attitudes, and preferences. Self-disclosure is of the essence of friendship; each person becomes vulnerable. I ask, "Will you accept me just as I am? Will I find that I am 'handled with care?' Will my dignity survive your gaze?"

Ignatius had a deep capacity for friendship, and he brought this into his relationship with God. I can likewise say to God, "God, you see me as a lover sees their dearly beloved. You wish only my good, and you want to share everything with me. Don't let me get in the way or resist."

I tell God about myself and how I am and about my dreams and difficulties. As Ignatius says, I make known my affairs to God and seek advice about them. I ask God for what I want and desire, and especially that everything about me may be directed purely to His praise and service.

As in all friendships, there are also companionable silences. It may seem that nothing is going on in this simple being-with-the-other, but heart is speaking to heart at a level too deep for words, and I am changed in the process.

So in summary, it won't do for me to report on my prayer by saying, "Well, I sit there and wait for something to happen, but it seldom does." Instead I try to talk out my issues with God and invite him to respond, which he does! This I-Thou approach can be uncomfortably revealing, I find. But it is worth it, and it eliminates the boredom I have often experienced in times of formal prayer.

When God Speaks

Some time ago I was helping a group of people to pray. My hope was to introduce them to the Jesus of the Gospels and then to stand back respectfully and let the relationship develop. So I read a scene from Jesus' life and invited them to get involved in it. I asked them to see Jesus looking at them individually, speaking directly to them, laying his hands on them, and so on. They caught on quickly and moved from being mere spectators to being participants. At the end, a man remarked, "That was really great. But it's a terrible pity they don't read that stuff in Church!" When asked to say more, he added, "This is the first time I felt the Bible is FOR ME. When it was read, it used to go over my head. It floated around but it never landed on me, and of course I wasn't expecting it would."

Scripture has to become personal if it is to have its intended impact. I need to hear Jesus speak face to face with me. "You are my friend, Brian." "Brian, go and sin no more!" "Brian, do not be afraid!" "Peace be with you, Brian!" "Brian, love others as I have loved you!" And so endlessly, Jesus addresses me in the second-person singular, and I am to respond in the same way. He is saying: "I want to talk with you, engage with you, heal you as really and directly as I did with those I met in Galilee." One word can suffice, as I know from meeting with Fr Pedro Arrupe, quoted in the frontispiece, after he had had a severe stroke and could speak only in monosyllables. I was on my way to work with refugees in Somalia in 1981, and I stopped in Rome en route to meet him. Refugees were very dear to him. He had only recently founded the Jesuit Refugee Service. I explained my mission. He gazed at me silently, then lifted his withered right hand and shouted "Go!" That single word kept me going in hard moments, and it thrills me still.

For the Christian, God's word is the Word of Life. It opens out for us the world of relationship between God and ourselves. Scripture reveals what God thinks of me, how God sees me, what God wishes for me, how I can play my part in the unfolding of God's divine project for the world. In the Gospels I am given in concrete and human form the example of how to live: I am to make my own the mind and heart of Christ Jesus. And that mind and heart are centred on the development of loving relationships between God, myself, and my neighbour.

Not to listen to God who is trying to speak to me is to restrict myself to a disoriented and hollow life. The glory of God is the human person fully alive, and I am brought to life by listening to God's word. So I pick a phrase or scene from the daily readings to nourish me in my prayer . . . "Lord, what are you trying to communicate to me today? I don't want to ignore you. Speak, Lord, your servant is trying to listen. You are not a distant God, but in touch with me today, at this hour. You are closer to me than breathing, and nearer than hands or feet. I may be all over the place, but you are with me always. I'm like a child engrossed in a game and don't hear my parent calling me. Take away my deafness and blindness. Make me a hearer of your word." By reading the Scriptures, I get to know God's mind on things; and when I respond, God in a sense gets to know my mind!

Prayer Has Already Begun

Andre Louf, in *The Cistercian Alternative*, makes the point that prayer is already going on at the heart of reality. I do not have to try in vain to contact a distant God. Prayer starts elsewhere than with me. The relationship of love between the Persons of the Trinity is eternally being expressed, and we rightly call it prayer. This prayer is their language. What I call my prayer is in fact God's. I am the holy place in which the divine Persons pray. St. Paul says that we do not know how to pray rightly, but the Holy Spirit makes the prayer deep within us (see Romans 8:26).

At the beginning, this prayer is below my consciousness. Slowly I am brought into it, as I was educated into the language of my parents by being lovingly and patiently taught. Think of adults dancing at a family party: you are the child, watching. The adults pull you in, and with the help of willing hands you gradually get into the rhythm. They are delighted with your performance, and over time you learn to dance well yourself.

Ignatius has often been accused of rigidity in setting out methods of prayer. While his instructions for beginners are concise, he never intended these to constrict further development. All he wanted to do was help people get directly in touch with God. And he showed them how to notice God. He then stepped aside, for he believed that the only teacher of prayer is the Holy Spirit and that God sees and knows what is best for each of us in our uniqueness. (See *Ignatius: Writings*, 206.)

As an aside, here it is good to note that Ignatius's respect for the inviolable relationship between God and the individual is echoed by C. S. Lewis's remark in *The Last Battle* that God tells no one any story but their own. We can spend long puzzling about other people and why they seem so insensitive to what is obvious to the rest of us. "Why can't he catch himself on?" "How is it that she just does not get it?" Perhaps God is saying to us, "Mind your own business. I'm at work here!" Our finding of God in these situations may be confined to the level of our faith.

Holy Waiting

It often seems to me that my prayer is a non-event. Nothing happens! I show up rather like a patient for radiation treatment: my hope is to become well, but I notice nothing during the treatment. But whatever has to be done, I want it, even if I have to endure much. And in the time of waiting which we call prayer, something is happening, deeper down than I can perceive. Such waiting is holy waiting, as is the season of Advent.

Very occasionally there occurs what the Welsh poet RS Thomas describes as "the movement of a curtain"—a tiny hint that God is attending and revealing something of his presence. Here is one description of God revealing himself more fully: for more, read the mystics! In 1487 a Carthusian monk was making his thanksgiving after Mass when, he says, God visited him in power, and he so yearned with love as almost to die. Love and longing for the Beloved raised him in spirit into heaven. As the pain of love grew more powerful, he formed within his spirit these words: "Love! Love! Love!" He could say no more.

For most of us, such moments as these are few, far between, and unexpected. But is that partly because we are inattentive and deaf? Is it also that God intends nothing less than *to give himself* to us, as Ignatius says? I might be distracted by lesser gifts. God is giving himself to me, deep down. St. Paul says that our inner nature is being renewed every day (2 Corinthians 4:16). Perhaps the most obvious sign of this "renewal" is that God is increasing in importance for me, while I become less important in my own eyes. I get caught somewhat less by situations that used to annoy me. I see something in scripture which I had passed by until now; I notice God's provident action in simple things, such as bumping into someone "by chance" and having a good encounter. In brief, I find God more often and more easily as the years go by.

SUGGESTED EXERCISE

- Settle into your preferred routine of time, place, and atmosphere.

- Notice how you feel, whether tired, energetic, peaceful, upset, focused, distracted . . .

- Greet Jesus when he arrives. Spend time on this, because the interpersonal quality of the first moments colour what follows. Hence it is better to say, "I am going *to meet the Lord*" than to say, "I am going to pray."

- Look over the Gospel of the day and see where you are drawn. (I am writing on Passion Sunday; the Gospel tells of the raising of Lazarus. The following is drawn from what happened for me as I prayed.)

- After Lazarus has been restored to his family and the crowd has moved away from Jesus, meet up with him in imagination and ask him what this miracle might mean for yourself.

- Jesus invites you into the tomb; it is dark and smelly. You can just about see him near you. "Lie down where Lazarus was," he says, "and ask yourself if there is anything about you that is dead or dying."

- You lie on the rock and feel the cold and discomfort . . . You think of your heart and soul, and areas where faith, hope, or love are only flickering rather than steadily burning. The glory of God is the human person fully alive, but you often feel only half-alive . . .

- You call out to him, "Lord, give me life, life in its abundance" (see John 10:10).

- How does he respond? Does he whisper words of comfort to you, perhaps touch you . . .? Allow him to take your hand, raise you up, and lead you out into the world of colour and pure air and birdsong . . .

- Praise and thank him. Don't spoil things by saying, "It's raining!"

CHAPTER 5

Informal Prayer

"Noisy Contemplation," "Prayer on the Hoof," "Prayer on the Wing," "Prayer as You Go," "Living Prayer," "Checking in with God"—call it what you like, there is a mode of informal relating with God that goes hand in hand with a spirituality that seeks to find God in all things. While formal prayer occurs when I set aside quality time for my encounter with God, informal prayer occurs while I am busy about other things but take a moment to bring God in.

Ignatius left his followers no hard and fast rule about the length of prayer. Instead he says, "Keep God always before your eyes!" It is so simple a statement yet seems so hard to achieve in the rush of life. But during a busy day, our desire for God does not disappear; it simply slips under our radar. Most Christians are good people whose fundamental option is to please God. But they are not thinking of God all the time. A good mother may be "a working mum" or looking after the house or an ageing parent. But even when busy about many things, she has an abiding sense of her husband and the children. All she does is for the good of the family. When she relaxes for a moment, the family spontaneously comes into her mind and heart, and she wishes them well. That is already an informal prayer, as the reflection immediately below reveals. When she turns her attention to

God, when she asks for help or thanks God for some lucky driving escape, this is "noisy contemplation."

I prayed a while ago this morning before I opened the computer, asking God to help me say something useful. But while writing now, I am not consciously thinking of God. Ideas come into my head. But from where? Let's suppose they are "good" ideas. If I believe, as the Church says, that all good things come from God, then can I, must I, not say that helpful ideas come from God, from the Good Spirit? That brings God alarmingly close! This links with a favourite anonymous reflection from the contemplative tradition, which warms my heart in cold times:

> "What each one is interiorly,
> face to face with God,
> unknown to anyone,
> is of vital consequence to all.
> And every act of love,
> every act of faith and adoration,
> every mute uplifting of the heart,
> raises the whole world nearer to God.
>
> From everyone who is in union with God
> there breathes a spiritual vitality, light, strength and joy,
> which reach from end to end of the universe;
> a source of grace to those least conscious of it,
> even to those least worthy of it,
> and knowing nothing of how and whence it comes."

I love the simplicity of this reflection! Without doubt formal prayer is important, but even small moments of goodness change the world for the better—the "little, nameless unremembered acts of kindness and of love" of which Wordsworth speaks. Are we then perhaps minor mystics, as I suggested in the Introduction? We are after all habitually set on God, even though we turn our attention to God only sporadically.

Meeting God in Nature

As with most people, I find it easy to see God in nature and beauty, and at least sometimes I speak to God about it, with gratitude and praise. In St. Ignatius's view, gratitude should become central in our lives, as we get to savour the goodness of God. For him, ingratitude was the greatest of sins, and he knew a variety of sins: he tells us that he took three days to make his confession after his conversion! He offers three hints on how we can cultivate a grateful heart.

First, he says, be grateful to God for creation. Most of us find this easy to do when we move beyond taking created things for granted. One of the great theologians of the last century, Hans Urs von Balthasar, speaks of creation as "the monstrance of God." The word *monstrance* means "pointing to," and a monstrance is used to hold the sacred Host when it is exposed on Catholic altars. The radiance of the monstrance draws the eye toward the treasure at the centre. The beauty of nature can do the same for us. As Hopkins puts it, "Give beauty back, beauty, beauty, beauty, back to God, beauty's self and beauty's giver" (From *The Leaden Echo and The Golden Echo, in Poems of Gerard Manley Hopkins*, ed W H Gardner. London: Penguin, 1984, 52).

Storms, earthquakes, and tsunamis spoil the perfect picture, of course. Our planet labours and undergoes startling upsets. Creation "groans in labour pains," as St. Paul says (Romans 8:22). But then he adds that we do the same ourselves, so we can learn to be patient with Mother Earth and with ourselves. For those who can see, there is a beauty in the imperfection of things, which is deeper than surface beauty. Witness the beauty in the struggle of a sick child or of a recovering alcoholic, in the tears of repentance or in the repose of death.

Next, I am called to be grateful for my redemption—for the fact that God should leave the world of the divine to rescue me in my distress. Why should I be infinitely loved, even unto death? Ignatius fell in love with the Jesus of the Gospels, who sacrificed his life for him in his wretchedness. For Ignatius, as for Pope Francis, the history of human life is a history of the mercy of God. God remains faithful in loving and serving me and invites me in turn into loving service of my fellow-sinners. An exclamation of grateful wonder is called forth in me for all of this. The illogical jump in the line, "I was helpless, so God saved me" (Psalm 116:6) has always appealed to me.

Lastly, I can be grateful for my particular gifts, my uniqueness, those special ways in which divine providence guides the course of my life. Sometimes I catch God in the act of looking after me, but usually it is only by reflection that I notice the action of providence. In all things, Ignatius affirms, God is like a lover who gives himself to his beloved. A grateful heart is born out of these multiple overwhelmings and these glad surprises. I find that in my spare time I reflect over what has been going on in my life, and I say in surprise to God, "Why are you so good to me? Why do you save me from all sorts of trouble, and why do you set up so many good things for me?"

Images of God Everywhere

Occasionally I see myself and other people as God's beloveds. This can both nourish and challenge me endlessly. How can that strange-looking, under-performing person who is irritating the life out of me be God's beloved! How is it that everyone in my bus is "a brother or sister for whom Christ died" (1 Corinthians 8:11)? I don't like crowds, but I can take a cue from St. Francis of Assisi, who saw crowds as "the image of God, multiplied but not monotonous."

Attending Meetings with God

When going to meetings I sometimes pray for the Spirit's help. I believe that meetings matter because decisions are to be made which affect the lives of others. I try—at least some of the time—to keep God's agenda in mind. More frequently now I drive with the radio off; the three divine Persons travel together with me. I ask them for wisdom: "What shall we do about this or that issue?" The Ignatian phrase "to love and serve in all things" jolts me out of passivity and inertia at boring meetings. It challenges the demon that says, "Brian, this is not your problem!" True, a refugee situation may not be my problem directly, but if we grant that all things are interconnected, God may want me to do something about it, not least to show interest and to pray. As St. Paul says, if one part of the body hurts, all the other parts should feel its pain (See 1 Corinthians 12:26).

Pray at All Times!

Jesus asks us to be alert and to pray at all times (Luke 21:36). My life is to be a living prayer. This can seem an impossible task because we have so much "living" to do. But Ignatian spirituality helps make it more manageable because it guides us into seeing that real Christian living is an open communication with God in everything that goes on. Everything speaks of God because all is related to God. There is no dualism between prayer and life: an undivided heart looks towards God in everything. God wants to be with us; he is always coming into our lives as they evolve. God wants us to involve him in every situation. The more you trust someone, the more you will share with them. Our energy for voice-mailing, texting, and tweeting shows how much we like to be in communication, and to share with God even a small detail is a life-giving experience for us; it is deepening of relationship, it is a prayer. God, after all, is endlessly communicating with us through every aspect of reality. All that surrounds me now—table, chair, computer, printer, paper, books, walls, pictures, carpet—all are instances of the spontaneous generosity of God. Ignatius saw God as untiringly provident, and so can I. The Jesuit Teilhard de Chardin titled his autobiographical sketch *The Divine Milieu* because he had caught on to the fact that God impresses Godself on us in all things. We who are minor mystics in training do well to spend odd moments imagining ourselves wrapped in the divine milieu!

An Involved God

Do you sense right now that God is involved in your life?

You may feel only half-alive, weak and sad, lost and alone, burdened and frightened. It can seem impossible to make a prayer within this miserable situation. God seems so distant that it would be impossible to reach Him: you haven't got the energy to search for Him. Is there such a thing as "Bad Form Prayer"?

Can you allow yourself to believe the amazing truth that God is passionately searching for you at this moment in the depths of the mess and despair? God knocks on your locked door, asking to be admitted into your life, offering to share your burden and to companion you through the darkness. Can you allow God to love you, to respect you, to give you back your integrity and your hope? Can you accept the dignity of being a friend of God and believe that this is one friendship that need never fail?

Did Jesus feel something like this in his Passion? How did he manage to keep going when everything seemed lost? He was helped by the fact that his whole life up to this point was a living prayer. In everything he did and in all that happened to him, he was looking out for his Father: they loved each other. He wanted so much to please his Father. The Father was the centre of his life, and this gave a fresh and wonderful meaning to everyone and everything in his world. Because he involved him in all he did, everything in his life, both the joyous and the painful, was a living prayer. So when everything fell apart and all seemed lost in the Passion, the centre still held firm. Father and Son were still together, still totally for one another. So it is for us: God is near, and God is involved on our side.

Love Is the Reason

Life can seem like an endless succession of tasks, some of them uncongenial. Where is God in the rat-race? For Ignatius, everything done with a pure intention of serving God is a living prayer. So a task we undertake in the sincere belief that this is what God wants is not less pleasing than private prayer. Seeking and finding God in all things is to be the primary issue for us, just as it was for Jesus. It leads to a life that is transparently open to God and available for whatever God wants. God and God's desires are put first, and the reason is love. The grace that enfolds our lives enables us to become fully what we are intended to be, the sons and daughters of God. "I will do these things in love and freedom or leave them alone" is a maxim from Mary Ward, Foundress of the Loreto Order, and I find it saves me from dragging grudgingly through my daily tasks. Space opens out, and there is ample room for what I am to do.

People who are busy for God, because God wants them to be busy, or also because they are ill, may not have much time for sustained prayer. Ignatius advises such people to take even some little moments to check in with God and to make sure that they are in harmony with God in their busyness: "Where are you, God, and where am I?" He even says that the practice of the Examen or "Examination of Consciousness" should take precedence over formal prayer if necessary. I have said something about this in *Reflective Living*.

SUGGESTED EXERCISE

- Can prayer be simpler than this dialogue? Allow God to speak your name when he responds to you.
- "Good morning, God!"
- "Good morning, my beloved . . ."
- "God, I come to you to take your touch before I begin my day. Bless me as I go!"
- "I will indeed! I have been watching over you as you slept, and now I will be with you however the day works out."
- (Some time later . . .) "Hello again, God!"
- "Thanks for being in touch. I'm always happy to hear from you. Don't forget that I gaze steadily on you and smile encouragingly, especially when things are bumpy for you! If you're stuck, let me know how I can help."
- (Later again . . .) "Good evening, God! I'm tired, but can we look over the day for a minute?"
- "Hi, my beloved. Yes, it's been quite a day for you, but you did your best and made some good things happen. Notice the small things. For instance, each time you smiled at someone, the world brightened up a bit for them. And you kept going even when you were under pressure. Now be nice to yourself and relax: I will sort out any mistakes you made. Sleep well!"
- "Thanks so much. See you in the morning!"

CHAPTER 6

"Imagine!"

The previous chapters will have made demands on your mind and heart. So let's take a short break and allow the right brain some scope! Images can help us grapple with all that is going on between God and ourselves. God has unlimited imagination; it is one of the innumerable gifts he shares with us. God is full of imaginative ideas about our development and communicates with us through images. Through good images we can find God. Here are three images that help me.

My first is of a tree trunk and a sculptor, and it comes from St. Ignatius, who got it from earlier writers. The second is the image of dancing; the last is of myself in moody moments. Let us look at these in turn.

A Miracle of Sculpture

Ignatius remarks:

> There are very few persons who realise what God would make of them if they abandoned themselves entirely into his hands and let themselves be formed by his grace.
>
> A thick and shapeless tree trunk would never believe that it could become a statue, admired as a miracle of sculpture, and would never submit itself to the chisel of the sculptor, who sees by his genius what he can make of it.

Many people who now scarcely live as Christians do not understand that they could become saints, if they would let themselves be formed by the grace of God and if they did not ruin his plans by resisting the work he wants to do.

(*Ignatius of Loyola: Letter to Ascanio Colonna*, Rome, April 25, 1543)

This image stresses how hard God has to work on us. God is the active one who labours ceaselessly in us till we become fully the images of God. Just as each snowflake, each fingerprint, is unique, each of us is an unprecedented and original image of God. That image is fleshed out through the unique history of each life. God is energetically at work on everyone at this task: the less promising a person might be, the more God works on them. Our role is to let God do his work, get in tune with it, support it, and never resist it.

This book is intended to help you catch on to the potential glory of you! At whatever stage of your journey you find yourself, you are being shaped and formed by God into the image of Jesus. This means becoming more and more open to God, until you possess God's fullness. Growth is from the inside out, from the depths of us to the surface. The outward sign that God is having his way with you is your growth in love.

The image of the sculptor at work hints at the pain entailed in our making. When the older liturgy referred to the formation of a priest, it spoke of God as shaping us "stroke by stroke" or "with many a wallop"—*tunsione plurima* for the Latinists!

The priest ought not to be like a statue of bronze, which is melted in a cast and which comes from the mould with the form which it will keep; but rather as a statue of marble, which is drawn laboriously from the block, stroke by stroke, and which must be carved and polished leisurely. (Louis Bacuez, *The Divine Office*. London: Herder, 1912, in the section on Minor Orders)

"With many a wallop!" It is a startling phrase: perhaps that is why it was dropped! But it is real: we are bruised by God's chiselling, and we feel it deeply. We can only believe that it is worth it. We can each say to God: I am not the person I would like to be, nor am I yet the person you would have me to be. This is not a terrible thing, just a realisation that you have more work to do in my heart. Help me to endure as you chisel off sharp edges and smooth rough corners. Let me be grateful to you that I am not the same person I was ten years ago, or even five. Please keep going!

A Dancing God

I met an accomplished teacher of dance recently, who confided to me that his partners often told him how well he'd danced. In response he would ask them if they had *enjoyed* the experience. Invariably they said, "Of course!" He knew that as the dance got under way and they shed their self-consciousness, they had become caught up in the dance. No longer passive, they had brought their own personalities to it, each of them uniquely. He had the gift of sensing their individuality as it expressed itself in subtle ways and was able to adjust effortlessly. "You know," he said, "somehow the dance was already in them!"

God is a dancing God: God approaches us one by one and asks, "May I have this dance?" God adjusts to my particular gifts and, even if I am flat-footed and uncoordinated, God brings it about that the dance becomes mine.

Note that my dance with God is not an exclusive event remote from everyone else. Rather, as the dance unfolds, God is signalling to me to invite other people in, because the divine dream is that God and all humankind will finally dance together. Leonardo Boff uses this image to describe the life of the world to come; note how everything is set in the plural. He writes:

At the end will be the festival of redeemed humankind. It will be the celestial dance of the freed, the banquet of sons and daughters in the homeland and household of the Trinity. In divinised creation we shall leap and sing, praise and love the Father, Son and Holy Spirit. And we shall be loved by them, praised by them, invited to dance and sing, sing and dance, dance and love, forever and forever. Amen.

(Leonardo Boff: *Trinity and Society.* NY: Orbis; 1992, 231)

Moody Moments

My third image is around the daily news. Bad news can lead me into dark moods. When I was younger, I was a thoroughgoing perfectionist, and I devoted much energy to the task of improving other people and occasionally even myself! Now I like to think of myself as a "burnt-out" perfectionist, yet I often find myself upset by all that goes wrong—in the environment, in people's lives, in my own ways of relating. It is here that Ignatian spirituality can lighten my darkening inner landscape.

Ignatius would say: "The world is indeed in a mess. Ask God what you ought to do about it!"

Perhaps one of the things God would invite me to do is say good-bye to the assumptions underlying perfectionism. Imperfection is in the nature of created things. God seems content with an imperfect world and even an imperfect Church. Surely God is also content with an imperfect me. "There is a crack in everything God has made" according to Emerson. And while Patrick Kavanagh would add that "through a chink too wide there comes in no wonder," it is through the cracks that the light shines in on our darkness. Jesus indeed tells us, "Be perfect just as your heavenly Father is perfect" (Matthew 5:48). But what he means is that we must develop the compassion God has for everyone, good and bad. We are to become "perfectly compassionate" because compassion is the nature of God and, because we are God's sons and daughters, we are to become like God in this way. The sacred is revealed in our experience of inadequacy and failure. "We all fall short," as St. Paul tells us. So the imperfection of one another is yet another arena in which we can find God.

Ignatius often ended his letters with a prayer that God would change us *from being weak and sad to being strong and joyous.*" Left to our inadequate selves, and sensitive to the pain and tragedy that distort our world, we would rightly be weak and sad. Ignatius himself used to speak of "the sad misery of this life." He too had his moods. But when we remind ourselves that God is powerfully engaged in everything around us and is inviting us to play our part in it according to our unique gifts and abilities, then we can begin to feel "strong and joyous."

Try picturing sadness and weakness on one side of you, and strength and joy on the other. What do they look like? Two dark and nasty figures on one side? Two luminous and smiling figures on the other? Don't loiter in no man's land between these opposites. Instead take strength and joy as your allies and move away with *determination*—a word Ignatius liked—from sadness and weakness. There you find God, strong and joyous.

SUGGESTED EXERCISE

- The Trappist monk, Thomas Merton, tells how one day God opened his imagination to see something that was there all the time but which he had never noticed before. He was standing in a busy shopping mall, watching people go by. Suddenly he saw "the secret beauty of their hearts, the depths of their hearts, the person that each one is in God's eyes." "If only," he says "they could all see themselves as they really are. If only we could see each other that way all the time . . ." (Thomas Merton: *Conjectures of a Guilty Bystander*. NY: Image, 1968, 158).

- Ask God to open *your* eyes to see his presence in the people you interact with daily. Allow yourself to enter the mystery of who each one is in God's eyes. Ask for a sense of wonder. Thank God for whatever is given to you.

- Remember how the blind man healed by Jesus first saw people "like trees walking." But when Jesus laid his hands on his eyes again, "he saw everything clearly" (Mark 8:22–15). So ask Jesus to lay his hands on your eyes.

- Resolve to practice this way of seeing people. It is the most immediate and easy way to find God in daily living.

CHAPTER 7

You Are Important!

We have talked about Ignatius's early life, in which he showed a deep awareness of his own importance. As a knight in armour, he believed that one person could make all the difference between victory and defeat. He had courage, and that gave him freedom to risk everything for what he judged to be important. Somebody who lately stumbled on Ignatius said to me, "I think Ignatius walked tall and free; when he saw what he wanted to do, he swished his cloak and went for it!"

Overwhelmed by Love

A recent study of the early companions of Ignatius reveals them to be a group of persons who were convinced of what they were about. They were confident and happy because they were overwhelmed by the realisation that the God of Jesus Christ was totally in love with them, totally for them, and that the only response to this was gratitude and a readiness to share this good news with others. These first exponents of Ignatian spirituality are described as engaged in a "ministry of consolation," which meant bringing others to a personal awareness of God's limitless love for them, and inviting them to the intimacy that escorts it.

How About You?

Do you believe that you are important to God, just as you are? Unless you do, it is difficult to get going and have the freedom and courage to risk everything for God, as Ignatius did.

Perhaps much of the passivity that lies heavy on the Church in our time is due to the fact that we have picked up the contrary message: that we are not important in the Church and in the divine scheme of things. Ignatian spirituality maintains that we are, first of all, totally and passionately loved, that God relates to us as the great lover who "gives and shares with the beloved what he possesses . . . and desires to give himself to me so far as he can" (*Ignatius: Writings*, 329).

The message we seem to have picked up is that we are, first of all, sinners, that we are objects of divine pity and that God cannot hope for very much from us. But if I believe that I am a problem to God, I become a problem to myself too. Life then becomes a heavy and joyless burden.

A Wayward Beloved

There are two truths here which must be seen in right perspective to one another: first, we are loved; second, we are sinners. Scripture opens its account of our relationship to God by stating that God creates us in his own image and likeness. God sees that we are very good. Later comes the account of the fall, but the loving continues: humankind is constantly being called back into loving relationship with God. We are indeed called to repent, to be converted, and never to despair.

St. Paul tells the Ephesians (1:4) that they were chosen before the foundation of the world, to be holy and blameless in God's sight and to live through love in his presence. In his letter to the Romans (chapters 5 and 8) he underlines the fact that, in spite of our failure to live up to the love shown us, divine love goes steadily on. It is poured into our hearts; it overwhelms us. Nothing can ever separate us from the love of God, and this is proved by the death and resurrection of Jesus.

Ignatius knew this: he knew what sinning was all about, and he refers frequently to the shame and horror he experienced as he became more fully aware of the fact that he was being loved in the middle of all his sinning. If he emerges as confident and happy after his conversion experience at Manresa in 1522, it is because he is aware of being lovingly sustained by God and of being welcomed into companionship with Jesus in his campaign for the establishment of a truly loving community of humankind.

Pope Francis lives out of the conviction that he is a sinner but that God shows him endless mercy. He also knows that God is choosing him for a particular work. His motto is, "Pitied and Chosen" (*miserando atque eligendo*). He is aware that for a long period in his life he acted in an authoritarian manner and hurt "hundreds of people." But God can be found hidden in human sinning, and now the memory of God's graciousness in his dark times gives him the energy to do great things for God. He comes across now as a free and humble man. He can show seemingly endless compassion to his fellow pilgrims because he himself has been forgiven and invited to move forward.

God Is Different

Ignatian spirituality, then, maintains that you are important to God and that you have a role to play in shaping the world around you. It maintains that you have unique gifts and creativity so that your role in the world will be uniquely yours.

We could spend a lifetime asking, "Why am I important to God?" It can seem an honest question but can hide a mistrust of God's goodness and then excuse us from the risk of engaging in the relationship. Whatever our bad experiences in human relationships, we need to allow God to be different, to be the One who can do nothing but love.

"As emeralds are green, so God is love." I am important to God because God chooses so. As a child I was important to my parents: to ask them "Why?" would be a wrong and hurtful question. It is simply so. Good friends are important to each other; husbands and wives are important to each other. For either to ask "Why?'" in a doubting way is to spoil the relationship. Love is the starting point and needs no justification.

Not Just "Holy People"

Do we believe that the reason for our creation is that there are three divine Persons at the heart of the world who love one another totally and who love us into existence and want us to be happy with them forever? Even if we say "Yes" to this question, the suspicion remains that God ends up loving only "holy people"—"good people"—and not sinners like ourselves.

Personal failings discourage us because we feel that God could not be with us in our mess. We doubt that God can understand how being in debt or becoming pregnant too soon can lead people to depression and thoughts of suicide. Surely God stays away from the world of drugs, child abuse, and casual violence?

A profound Ignatian insight can help us as we search for God in the underside of life. This insight is hidden in the simplest of words: "*for me*" and "*with me*." Ignatius lived in the era of Spanish chivalry, when the relationship between a knight and his lord was idealised as one of unbreakable partnership. They would share the hardships and the glory of the campaign, and either would die for the other if need be. On his sick bed in Loyola after the failed campaign at Pamplona, Ignatius fell in love with the Lord of all things, who, he said, "had suffered and died *for me*." "*For me*" echoes St. Paul's cry of joy and wonder: "He loved me and delivered himself *for me*" (Galatians 2:20). We too can understand Jesus as the Incarnate Lord who enters the fearful side of the human condition, and he does it *for love of me*. He then invites me to share in his campaign to build the world that God dreams of. "Come *with me*, labour *with me*, share the glory *with me*," he says. No matter how demanding the campaign becomes, he will be there in the thick of things, and he looks around for my companionship.

"I Am with You!"

Ignatian spirituality tells us that we are not alone, that God is not removed from our world. The task is not so much about getting out of the mess to find God but about bringing God into the mess. God meets us in our personal experience, in our relationships, dreams, hopes, pain, and worries. Because everything about us is important to God, our life experience is the place where God encounters us. God relates with us through others but also directly. It is by reflecting on our personal inner experience that we become aware of *what's really going on for us*, rather than what appears on the surface of our lives. "What's going on?" can be superficial, but "What's really happening?" reaches to the depths where God is silently at work.

While Ignatian spirituality is intensely personal and intimate, it would be wrong to interpret it as individualistic. Just as the relationship between Jesus and his Father overflows into limitless love for all humankind, so for Ignatius. Being important to God will involve being available for the service of God's other friends who need our help.

SUGGESTED EXERCISE

- You are taking a well-earned rest after work, dozing. Imagine a knock at the door. You become more alert, wondering who is there. Perhaps the dog barks or the cat wakes up. On your way to answer the knock you may tidy some papers that are strewn around, glance in the hall mirror to make sure you are presentable. You are wondering, anticipating: who can it be?

- On opening the door there is a definite change of feeling, change of experience. If it is someone you know and love, and if the visit is a surprise, it is such a good feeling.

- Imagine opening the door and finding Jesus standing there, smiling. What feelings take over in you? You may be a bit overcome. He is so special; there has never been anyone like him in your life before. Why, you wonder, would he want to spend time with you?

- But there he is, asking if he may come in. You usher him in along the hall, sit him down, ask what you can get him. You fix a little snack while you're wondering, "What will I say to him that would interest him?"

- But soon you find yourself chatting easily with him. Everything in your life seems to mean something to him. He has the knack of opening things up to reveal their hidden meaning . . .

- At the end of such a meal you are changed because Jesus and you have spent some time together. The conversation between you somehow alters the way you've been seeing the things you have talked about.

CHAPTER 8

What's God Like?

I used to visit an older person who was in the throes of dementia. On one occasion she asked me to help her find something she had lost earlier in the day. I asked, "What are we looking for?" She smiled, went blank for a while, and then said, "I've forgotten!"

It helps then to know what we are looking for when we are looking for God! If you were asked, "What is God like?" what would you have to say? Don't we find it hard to talk about God? Yet in each of us there is a deep longing to know God. If you put the question to Ignatius of Loyola, he would stop, smile, maybe shed tears—as he often did when he thought about God. Then he might say, "How long have you got?" and begin to share with you something of his own long journey of growing in appreciation of God.

Ablaze with God

As we have said above, Ignatius was a thirty-year-old before he became aware that God was intending to take up residence in the centre of his life. Only when his life came to an abrupt halt did he stop to think more deeply about things and wake up to the astonishing fact that God was passionately interested in him, in love with him. In the intimacy of long contemplation, Ignatius grasped at a very deep level that the life, passion, and resurrection of Jesus were all for him.

He struggled to the startling awareness that his life must be important to God. This gave a whole new meaning to his life and choices. He became aware that God was present in his experiences, that there was no dividing line between life and prayer but that God was constantly speaking to him in his ordinary living: nudging, challenging, helping, beckoning, opening up new undreamt-of vistas of love and service. In a brief phrase in his *Autobiography* he lets us in on what was happening between himself and God: he was becoming "a generous spirit, ablaze with God" (*Ignatius: Writings*, 16).

What God Is Not

Like ourselves, Ignatius had to work through narrow images of God to get to richer ones. He would have rejected the idea that God is a lonely celestial watchmaker who has wound up the universe and got it going and who leaves it now to tick away and run down by itself. Likewise, he had to discard the picture of God as a wise and serious judge or an accountant with a frighteningly accurate memory and a red pen, who watches out for our mistakes.

Moving on to a deeper level, he would sympathise with our tendency to think of God as the interfering controller. Caught in this image, we find it so hard to take the risk of exposing our needs and brokenness to God. We do not easily trust that God is simply good and always on our side.

We struggle to keep God at a distance so that the darker side of ourselves will not be seen. Ignatius was aware of how we battle to make God fit in with our narrow plans, how we try to control and tame God and make him "neat and fit for purpose." But he would say to us that by trying to domesticate God we remove the anticipation of being surprised by God. If we opt for peace and security and a quiet life, everything becomes ordinary and pedestrian and "safe." We lose the sense of awe, wonder, and mystery—all part of our being created.

The colour and vibrancy of life are lost to us and we live in a world of faded dreams: God becomes simply one object among many in a dull world, and all of this occurs because we think of God as threatening to spoil our joy. If we operate with this distorted image, then we limit God's creative influence in our lives.

The Gracious Lover

Ignatius proposes an opposite image to the above: it is the image of *The Gracious Lover*! From experience he asserts that when we take the risk of letting God be God—and it is a risk—the lights go on and life flows. God indeed becomes surprising, but the surprises are good rather than frightening. When we let God work freely, rather than spend our energies trying to avoid him, then we bump into him everywhere and each mysterious encounter evokes awe, wonder, and joy.

Instead of restricting God, we now find ourselves begging God to work in us and through us. Our dreams take on a new freshness because they are the dreams of God. God becomes the centre of an endlessly fascinating world, and the deepest desire of our hearts is to find God in everything rather than to limit him in any way.

What do we find when we "find" God in the here and now? Perhaps we take it for granted that we know. "Finding God" is not like discovering a missing person or finding an answer to a problem or unearthing a crock of gold at the end of a rainbow. God is not sitting on top of a hill or peering out from the petals of a rose. God is indeed transcendent, but also *immanent*. "Immanent" means "residing in." God is *not apart* from the hill or the rose. God "resides in" or "inhabits" our creation. God is not separate and apart from the directors in the board room or the students in the classroom. God is in the nurses in the hospital and also in those who are afflicted mentally or physically.

God is in the reality of all persons, situations, and things, while remaining unknown. We can't identify the face of God in a crowd in the way we can identify an Irish or a Nigerian face. I cannot *prove* that I have found God, and yet I know sometimes that I am meeting with a reality that is deeply satisfying and fulfilling. What nourishes the deepest level of my being is divine.

All Is Sacred

I walk a sacred world. Nothing is "profane"—the word *fanum* meant a shrine, so "profane" originally meant "outside the shrine," that is, outside the place where the divinity resided. But the human story and the material universe itself are sacred because of the Incarnation. Creation is the monstrance of God. The footprint of God is to be found everywhere. Most encouragingly, God is present in evil, *working to bring good out of it*. This we know from the passion, death, and resurrection of Jesus. Because we forget so easily that God is labouring for us in the dark dimension of life, the Eucharist is present to remind us. He commands us to "Do this in memory of me." Eucharist reminds us of how God turned evil inside out, revealing a love that we could never have dreamt of. God is never fully revealed to us in this life, but when we experience joy, love, beauty, truth, peace, goodness, energy, and clarity, we are right to say that God is around. Whatever is life-enhancing and good comes from God.

Sharing God's Dream

God is Trinitarian: there are three mysterious but totally good and infinitely resourceful persons at the heart of our world. Because they love us unconditionally, they watch over our lives with infinite care and engage with us in every detail. In one way, they are far ahead of us as they plan and labour for our good. From another point of view, they walk and work with us, guiding, supporting, sharing our burdens, and keeping us going. They have a project to which they are totally committed: their dream is to bring all humankind to joy, the final community of love. They reveal this dream so that we may participate in its completion.

For Ignatius, then, God is dynamic, eternally active, always making the first move. Ignatius's favourite term in reference to God is "The Divine Majesty," the Lord of all history and of all creation. Each person, he believed, is needed to bring to completion what God has in mind. Further, God is endlessly provident and supplies us, as his trusted co-workers, with everything we need for the tasks given us. We have only to ask!

God Meets Us in Love

While God certainly blesses us richly with all we need for our tasks, Christian living is not to be reduced to simply working for God. The service or work must flow from awareness of being loved by God and by loving in return. God is the Lover who shares with the beloved what he possesses; he is the Lord who "desires to give himself to me." For Ignatius, personal relationship with God is central and life becomes a journey into limitless levels of intimacy and friendship with him. The quality of this loving relationship is dependent only on our openness to it.

Here Ignatius might pause and say, "I have said enough! The simplest and best way to get to know what God is really like is to speak with Jesus exactly as one friend speaks to another." And so, to the exercise that follows.

SUGGESTED EXERCISE

If you have followed the earlier exercises, you will be growing in ease in talking with Jesus.

- Now imagine yourself sitting with him and chatting. A companionable silence follows.

- Then it comes into your mind to ask him about his Father. You already know something about his mother, but his Father . . .?

- So you say, "What is your Father really like?"

- He replies, "You probably think that my Father is very different from me?"

- You might say, "Yes, I feel comfortable with you, and I love what I have learnt about your openness, your willingness to take risks, your desire to bring me life, your friendship. I've come to know that you really do see me as your friend, that you understand me and my life. But does your Father understand and love me in the same way?"

- He smiles. "Yes. This is just the point! My Father and I are alike. You know the way we say, 'Like father, like son?' It's absolutely true in our case. I just try to reveal him; I make his love visible and concrete. We Three—I am including the Holy Spirit here—love you infinitely."

- A rich silence descends. I allow myself to be bathed in the awareness that, despite all my inadequacy, I am limitlessly loved by the three divine Persons. Their care for me is boundless. I am the focus of the unpredictable liberality of God!

CHAPTER 9

Where Love Is, There Is God

Religion Is a Love Affair

We are made for relationships! At the heart of our being is God's loving relationship with us, and our response to that. Some streams of spirituality emphasise religious practices and rules rather than the personal experience that underlies and gives meaning to them. That God is to be found in particular practices is certain: so the Mass, Communion, the sacrament of Reconciliation, devotion to the Sacred Heart, the Rosary—all such practices can promote the vitality of our Faith.

Surveys, however, reveal that in Ireland, at least, we have been strong on the institutional level of faith, but weak on the mystical level. This means that many Irish Catholics have little sense that God is in love with them and they with God. Personal experience of our relationship with God needs to be emphasised. Here is where Ignatian spirituality helps, because it stresses that we can experience God in a one-to-one relationship and also find God in our mundane experiences. Our religious practices, whether the Eucharist, vocal prayer, or whatever, nourish us best when they flow from and express our relationship with God. When you are in love, you find all sorts of ways of showing it: some ways will be structured and others spontaneous. When we were younger, perhaps we sometimes confessed, "I didn't get my prayer in" or "I didn't get to Mass," as if loving God and meeting up with him were simply an obligation. No! We go to prayer or to Mass to meet God, who is there for us. That little word "for" sums up God's attitude toward us. Father, Son, and Spirit are "for us" and invite us to be "for" one another, so that in the long run God and humankind will form one loving community in which everyone is "for" everyone else.

Experiencing Relationship

A woman said to me recently, "All my life I've been involved in doing deals with God. I fancied that if I said a certain number of prayers or performed tasks in set ways, then God would give me what I had earned. I've spent a long time explaining my life to God!"

When I asked her what she meant, she said, "I thought it had to be all hard work and serious faces, a grinding slog. Now I've come to see Jesus standing in front of me—perhaps smiling a little wryly—waiting for me to stop working so hard at prayer, willing me to pause for breath, to take time to lift my head and look at him, just to give him a chance to speak."

"He lets me know that he understands about feelings, the loving and laughing, the loss and sadness. Events, including sex, don't have to be sanitised before I share their joy with him; the eyes don't have to be dried and the smile fixed on! He might indeed shed a tear with me (and for me) if I could allow it. And I've also learned that he doesn't blush as easily as I thought he might, which is comforting!"

Centre of Her Life

This woman is catching on to her personal experience of God, and she's finding the relationship between herself and Jesus warm and real. If she lets it unfold, she will find this direct and intimate relationship with God becoming more and more the centre of her life. It is wonderful to her that an ordinary person like herself is known and loved directly by God and that she can know and love him directly too. But she told me she fears that if she lets the relationship develop, she herself will be changed and she may lose contact with the other people in her life. She feels it is an either/or situation: either God or the people in her life.

But a great richness of Ignatian spirituality is that it helps us both to cultivate our relationship with God and recognise that God is in all our other relationships. And not only is God in our human relationships, he is also in all our experiences of life. According to Ignatius, we are to love God in all things, and all things in God. Nothing, absolutely nothing, is to fall outside the world of love.

God is most certainly in our relationships. The world of grace into which we are invited is a world of relationships, and so God's work with us centres on the developing of relationships. The three divine Persons, who relate so lovingly with one another, want to extend their love to everyone. Therefore, when we are loved and love one another, we experience that relating love and, in this way, we experience God as present in all our human relationships.

Where love is, there God is! In experiencing love in daily life, we are in fact experiencing God: when we experience that love as absent, we find in ourselves a yearning for it, and that yearning is a desire for God. "To love another person is to see the face of God"—so goes the final song in *Les Miserables*. C. S. Lewis in *The Four Loves* expresses the same truth as follows: "When we see the face of God we shall know that we have always known it. He has been a party to . . . all our earthly experiences of innocent love."

God in Our Life Experiences

Can it be true that God is to be found everywhere? In holy places and in the kitchen? In school and in the waiting room? In examination halls and interview rooms? In the income tax office and in the unemployment office? In parks and at the seaside? In police stations and courtrooms? In emergency rooms and maternity wards? In traffic jams, supermarket check-outs, and the disco? In other words, can we find God in our day-to-day reality?

Some spiritualities doubt that God is present in our ordinary human experiences, but Ignatian spirituality holds that God wants to be found in the flesh and blood of everyday life, just as he wanted to be found in the flesh-and-blood person named Jesus. Just as Jesus met his Father in the day-to-day experiences of his life, so can we. This is why Ignatian spirituality is termed an *incarnational* spirituality: it is en-fleshed. Each of us is an en-fleshed spirit, and we encapsulate a whole history and a wealth of experiences: within these we can search for God and be sure of finding him.

SUGGESTED EXERCISE

- Sometimes you have only a short space of time in your day for prayer: you could spend it in vocal prayer or in meditating on a passage of Scripture. This is good, but Ignatius, because he was so convinced that God is right beside us in the events of our day, suggests that you give the time over to reflecting on what is going on for you in your life right now. God is to be found in all your experiences, and if you stand back with him, he will help you notice how he is present in them.

- So, settle down, perhaps in your friendly chair, and pull up another one for Jesus. Review the day with him, noticing with his help all the good that was in it. Let gratitude well up in your heart.

- But perhaps a bad event dominates your reflection: you had a row with someone and it ended badly. You realise that you were tired, and you know that when you are tired you are irritable. You also realise that you had been bottling up lots of anger rather than being more truthful earlier on. So you exploded.

- You ask Jesus to teach you "just as a schoolmaster teaches a child" (Ignatius's phrase about himself being taught by God). You want to find a way towards a more authentic relationship, even if it involves painful honesty. You decide to pray for the other person, and for yourself, and to watch out for that tiredness in the future!

- Jesus encourages you. "It's not easy!" he says. "I was pretty sensitive myself, and I often found it hard to control my anger too."

- End by entrusting this difficult relationship to his healing grace.

CHAPTER 10

God of the Chaotic

Everywhere a God-Zone

Ignatius refers to Jesus as "the Eternal Lord *of all things*." Since God is Lord of all things, God can be found in all things, in the medley of events and experiences that constitute everyday life. God is to be found both when I am at Mass and when I miss it, when I am pious and when I am addled, when I am devout and when I am having a drink. The unemployed are no less valued by God than those who are blessed with work. Sexuality and family life are sacred places to meet God, no less than celibacy. Everywhere is a God-zone: all those bits of our lives that seem meaningless in themselves are given meaning by God within the vast story of human history.

A Week in the Life

It's time for a story, so let's look in on an ordinary family during a week full of things that "just seemed to happen" to them. We'll stay with Ann, the mother, as she looks back when it is over and discovers, to her surprise, that she hadn't been alone. God was there!

On Sunday evening her son visited, and his parents were glad to see him. He is twenty-two, has studied English at university but has now decided to work as a cleaner until he sells his first novel. He moved out last year. Casually, while sitting at the table on Sunday, he said he hoped to go back to university. His mother's heart missed a beat. She had always wanted him to get a proper job: could this be the answer? But he had no money and needed the application fee. With some mis-givings—he smoked and drank any spare cash he had—his parents gave him the money.

Who Could It Be?

Each Monday, Ann meets some friends to pray. On that particular night one of the group recounted the story of the abbot whose monastery had been famous for its holiness. But hard times had come, and people no longer flocked there to nourish their spirit; the stream of young aspirants had dried up, the church was silent. Only a few sad and lonely monks remained.

When the abbot asked advice of a holy man, he was told that the situation had come about because of ignorance: one of the monks in the monastery was the Messiah in disguise, and nobody recognised this fact.

Such excitement when he told his story to his companions! Imag-ine having the Messiah living with them. Who could it be? The holy man had said that the Messiah was in disguise, so each person's defects, clearly visible to all the others, had to be part of the disguise. Since they realised that they could not recognise him, they took to treating each other with great respect. After all, one never knew . . .! The monastery was very soon filled with joy and love.

Ann loved the story and came home smiling. She was only in the door when her son rang to say he had lost his wallet that day: the money they had given him was in it.

And So It Goes

On Tuesday, the ignition in their old car let them down. On Wednesday, the car had to be fixed and Ann's mother was taken ill. And so the week went on.

On Thursday, a little boy who lives on the road stuck a wire into the lock on the car boot, so it was impossible to stow the supermarket shopping.

Friday was like the other days: it rained all day. The bus came too near the path and splashed dirty water over Ann's new coat. While these things were happening, the deeper problems of life remained to be coped with. Relationships still needed care, and someone close to Ann was going through a bout of bad depression. The hunger-filled eyes of refugee children stared out at her from the TV, and the question floated around in her mind: "Would the money, now lost, which we gave our son, have been better sent to help these starving children?"

When Saturday came, Ann got the lock on the car fixed. Later that morning, they had two callers to the door asking for money; she gave what she could.

Not Another Knock!

In the early afternoon there was yet another knock. Looking out from an upstairs window, she saw a very old man. Her heart sank. "Not another sad story!" she prayed. She whispered to her husband not to open the door. They waited. There was another knock. Her husband looked at her quizzically. "But you always answer the door," he whispered. Another knock, fainter now; the man was leaving. Husband and wife nodded to each other and he opened the door.

The old man turned and asked for their son by name. "He doesn't live here now," her husband said, "but perhaps I can help." "I found his wallet on Monday last," the old man said, "and I waited until the weather improved to bring it to the address on his student card."

He came in and sat down and took a drink of fizzy orange. At eighty-four, he was in good health and a great reader, though he had had little formal education. He thought that the loss of the library cards which he found in the wallet would be more important to the young man than the money. He held the young man's photo in his hands for quite a while and remarked: "He'll be OK."

God Has Been Busy

When the old man left, Ann and her husband were silent for a while: both had a sense that something mysterious was going on. Out for a walk together, they went over what had happened. Ann had lived out her week in blind faith: it was one of many similar weeks, and she'd felt puzzled at times at the lack of joy in her world. She knew she was trying to find God, but sometimes, and for long periods, God seemed to be hiding—or even lost!

Now the old man's kindness was bringing a first glimmer of light and hope. She began to make connections. If their son hadn't been as he was, he wouldn't have needed the money; therefore he wouldn't have lost it, and so the old man would never have come into their lives. Now the wallet was back, their son was affirmed by the old man, and husband and wife were drawn closer by all that had happened.

Even the old man had been helped. He had gone out of his way to respond when God had nudged him, but he had enjoyed meeting the family because he was a lonely man. Ann felt a sense of mystery pervading the panorama of the week, and she is now finding it easier to say, "God is busy behind the scenes, and I know it!" Other events of that week still don't make any sense, but there are times when she can say, "I often don't know why things happen, but it's all right."

Her hope can survive chaos because she is catching on to the fact that God really does understand us and can bring good out of the messiness of our lives. She's almost daring to address him now as "God of the chaotic and the unfinished"! She also knows that the Messiah called to their house that Saturday!

SUGGESTED EXERCISE

- Once again, find that place in which you can be quiet and where you are not likely to be disturbed for a while; sit or walk, and talk with Jesus.
- Tell him about your past week. Share with him how the days and nights unfolded, whether they were wonderful or not so good.
- The sharing of your memories and reflections with a friend who has all the time in the world to listen to you will be good.
- Ask Jesus to help you see where he was in the living and loving, the discussing and arguing, the laughing and crying, the rushing and working, or, perhaps, in the enforced sitting or the lying still.
- Speak as you would to someone who you know loves you, just as you are. The more regularly you do this, the more you will be convinced how absolutely dependable Jesus is. He is there for you, as he promised.

CHAPTER 11

When God Seems Deaf

Talking with God is good: it brings a depth of reality into my relationship with him. But in times of difficulty, I often complain to God that he is silent. "Here I am, needing help, and you do nothing, you say nothing. And if I am out of favour with you, can't you at least help the innocent person for whom I am interceding?" It happens that as I am writing this, I have just lost an important key: I have searched "everywhere." I am distracted and worried. A tiny whisper from above would surely spoil no great eternal plan! But God is off the line, away on holiday, divinely deaf.

God's silences test my faith. But since there is no one else to call on, I have to continue to badger him relentlessly like the woman Jesus commends who finally gets the attention of the corrupt judge (Luke 18:1-6). Even when God eventually answers such screams, it may be to send me the opposite of what I want. While sometimes that may turn out for the best, it seems not to at the time. Wars and genocides, diseases and great suffering, the Holocaust—such events bring us to a crossroads: do we continue to search for God or abandon what had been a promising relationship? Likewise, when prayer grows dry and "nothing works"—What to do? Often we can only echo Jesus' lament of abandonment on the Cross: "Why have you forsaken me?" (Matthew 27:46). Occasionally we find that, exhausted and spent, we have been carried to a new place, as the psalmist describes in the latter half of this psalm. The threatening black void of unbelief yields to the mystic darkness of faith. God's message seems to be: "No matter what goes wrong, don't lose faith in me!"

Because finding God often involves an encounter with something surprising, my searching must have an open quality about it. If I think of God as only light and joy, I shall search only there, and so I limit God. God may choose to be in dark and forbidding places, and on our pilgrim way we often find God so. God is shown as the serene and majestic creator in the beginning of Genesis. But God is revealed so differently in Exodus, under the images of thunder, lightning, earthquakes, plagues. The poor Hebrews were so terrified to bump into God in this way that they begged to be spared any further revelation! Likewise, God speaks with Job, but out of a whirlwind. He speaks to Elijah too, but not through the wind, the earthquake, the fire. "After the fire was the sound of sheer silence" and then the Lord spoke (1 Kings 19:11–13). God can appear in many guises, including darkness. We can find God in the desert too: "I (the Lord) will allure her and bring her into the wilderness, and speak tenderly to her" (Hosea 2:14). Finally, because as Son of God Jesus appears as a carpenter, the Jews found it almost impossible to recognise him. When in the Passion he became disfigured and "no longer human," only pure faith could recognise him as divine. So we do not rightly know what we are looking for when we search for God: we must let him reveal himself as he will. Yet in some deep place we know when we have found him, whether in darkness or in light.

In a recent document, the Jesuits emphasised for themselves and their associates that commitment to the service of faith and the promotion of justice can bring us to our limits. Thirty years ago, I was in Somalia and I toured the only hospital in the region. There I encountered a young woman with an obviously sick child in her arms.

Wordlessly she begged me for medicine, but of course I had none to give. A colleague later suggested to me that I had been simply "a tourist of misery" in the situation, doing neither the child, the mother, nor myself any real good. Angry first and then shocked, I began to reflect on what he said. I came to an abiding shame for what the Eastern and Western powers had done to Somalia. And that was humbling and good. More recently, at a rally for those who had endured clerical sexual abuse, I was shredded by a victim who discovered I was a priest. "But I'm innocent!" I said. "So was I before I was abused by the likes of you!" he replied.

In human anguish, the Jesuit document goes on, "the divinity is hidden"—Ignatius's phrase about Jesus in his Passion. Here occurs our experience of a hidden God. But even in the depths of darkness, when God seems concealed, a transforming light may shine. God labours intensely in this hiddenness. Rising from the tombs of personal life and history, the Lord appears when we least expect him. He comes as a friend bringing personal consolation, and as the centre of a servant community. From evil emerges some good, if only we can notice.

Finding God in Difficult Persons

"Charity begins at home," we say, and so finding God must include finding him in my awkward neighbour. There is plenty of raw material here! Only for brief periods are all our relationships harmonious. Nearly always there is at least one person who is making life hard for us. It is as if God sets things up so that when one pest goes, another, perhaps even more disagreeable, takes their place. But how can I find God in those "impossible people" whom I neither love nor like?

To find God in these twisted relationships, let us start by imagining someone you find difficult. Next, imagine Jesus coming to this person, smiling a loving gaze at him or her. They are probably unaware that they are loved by God, but God loves them anyway, without conditions. Jesus then comes over to you, sees the look on your face, and chats with you. "Yes, I do love this person," he says. "This is my brother or sister for whom I died. I simply love everyone as the Father loves me—totally."

You think on this for a bit, then say, "But *what* can I love in them?" Jesus responds: "I'm not saying it is easy to love them. But a few things can help. I love them with what I call *agape-love*. It's a love that is committed to you, no matter what. That is how I love you, you will be glad to know! Once you see that this is how you are loved, it gets a bit easier to love others in the same unlimited way. Your own shortcomings encourage you to cut a bit of slack for others with their imperfections. I keep my eye on the deep down good in you, and I see your potential. Remember that we talked of taking a long, loving look at the real? It's like the sculptor with the statue! Look at this 'pest' in a contemplative way. Pray for them, don't treat them as impossible. I haven't given up on them yet, nor on you! Actually, no one is 'impossible' to God, even though they seem to be so for you. Instead of raging at them, channel that energy into praying for them that God's goodness may be more and more in them. That's what I used to do, especially in my last hours. And pray the odd prayer for yourself too!"

You reflect in silence, then mutter, "I can't do this on my own. Please expand my small and miserable heart till it's more like your own."

"I will," he says. "Thanks for wanting this. Only by growing in love for others do you become a daughter or son of God. I work hard so that everyone may reach their full potential and become totally loving. But you play your part in this divine work. Your inadequacies challenge those around you to grow in love. In turn, their failings challenge your heart to grow by accepting them. And so it goes. It is, I admit, a long-range operation, but human flaws are the passageway to a more loving heart!"

He smiles at me in the silence. I say, "Jesus, you're so different from me! Is this the dynamic behind so many of our human interactions, that you involve us in polishing each other? And does it mean that at the End I'll be grateful not only to my friends but also to my enemies for pushing me into the world of love?" He smiles. "You're catching on! Remember the prayer one of my own race wrote in the death camp at the time when six million of us were exterminated?"

> Lord, when you enter your glory, do not remember only people of good will. Remember also those of ill will. Do not remember their cruelty and violence. Instead be mindful of the fruits we bore because of what they did to us. Remember the patience of some and the courage of others. Remember the camaraderie, humility, fidelity and greatness of heart which they awoke in us. So when they come to judgement, O Lord, grant that the fruits we bore may one day be their redemption.

(This anonymous prayer was found pinned to the clothing of a victim of the gas chambers of Ravensbruck, during World War Two. The atmosphere of this women's concentration camp is captured by Corrie Ten Boom in *The Hiding Place*. A Dutch woman, she had committed "the crime of loving Jews." The book is a tribute to the capacity of some of the victims to find God in the horror around them).

I say quietly, "Thanks. I think that will keep me going for a bit in the task of finding God in my neighbour!"

SUGGESTED EXERCISE

- Find your most helpful place to be with Jesus. Imagine you have greeted one another and settled down. You say to him, "I'm going through a tough time," and you tell him what's happening in your life.

- "Perhaps it may help if we go back to Calvary for a bit?" he says. "Imagine it is now. Picture all of humankind shuffling along below that little hill, each person carrying their burden of pain and suffering. I'm there, on the Cross. That's where I want to be, in a way, raised on high so people can see me and draw strength from me."

- "How?" I ask.

- "Well, for those who can see, I am a sign that God knows suffering from the inside. God is right beside them. I'm there waiting for them to come by. Why? Because the Lover is always looking out for the beloved, and I love them all. So I want to be where they must pass. I'm on the same Way of the Cross, the same *via dolorosa* they are on. That's a comfort to those who look up and see."

- "What about the others? So many are looking down in despair, and some are looking in the opposite direction . . ."

- "True," he says, "and that's why I need people like you to spread the news, so as to help these people. Tell them I meet them in their anguish, that I hold them and weep with them. I can strengthen them. Imagine they each met someone along the way who loved them. Wouldn't that cheer them? And if they knew that this person loves them limitlessly and could carry their grief and transform it into something worthwhile, wouldn't that help them?"

- We fall silent for a while, then I express what is in my heart, and we say farewell to each other.

CHAPTER 12

Decisions! Decisions!

Where Are We?

Let's pause at this stage of our exploring to see where we are. We began by noting how God can be found in formal prayer but also during the daily routine of things. We looked at a surprised Ignatius as he came to realise that he was very important to God. We saw that this is likewise true of us. We noted that God invites us to untold personal intimacy with himself as well as to task and service. We came to see that we can make a difference in a needy world, especially now that we know that God is with us. With this right sense of self-worth we began to wonder what God's dream for us might be. We sketched out an image of this dreaming God as dynamic, creative, loving, and ceaselessly active in our distorted and wounded world.

We focussed on how the three divine Persons invite us to be co-workers in the carrying through of their project, which is to salvage our chaotic human history. We surveyed how prayerful reflection can discover God not only in "religious" events but in our relationships and our everyday experiences, whether they appear graced or godless.

What is emerging is that Ignatian spirituality is a journeying one. For much of his life Ignatius was a journeyman, a traveller, a pilgrim. Not only did he walk the roads of Europe but he also struggled on the paths of the inner journey where a person encounters God. In all of this, Ignatius was breaking from the monastic tradition in which life is tightly ordered so that a monk may find God more easily in the unchanging pattern of his day. Ignatius instead heads for the open world where God is found not by external rules but by an inner compass that searches for God wherever he may be. As you, the reader, allow yourself to be caught by this kind of spirituality, you find that your own personal journey is underway.

Because your trust in God and your sense of being important to God are both growing, you are more willing to take risks. The willingness to take risks involves a sense of your own freedom and a desire to use it for whatever seems best: you find yourself wanting to follow the prompting and beckoning of a companioning God rather than staying "at home" with what is safe and predictable.

Personal Choice

So we come to the task of finding God in our decisions. Life is an endless series of choices, and we are free to make them as we will. This freedom is God's ambiguous gift to us—liberty can lead us onto the right path or badly astray. The human journey is not mapped out beforehand: in fact, there is no map and no road until we make our choice and set out. Someone has conjectured that perhaps eighty-five million meetings occur daily, and that in each of them decisions are made which may have implications on innumerable people, whether alive now or yet to be born. High-level meetings about the environment and climate change are an obvious example. But insofar as a common concern is missing, meetings can fail dreadfully. Left to itself, humankind is incapable of sustained development and order. There is however a divine solution to the problem of bad choices. It is simple but demanding. It is found in the life and teaching of Jesus and in making his mind and heart our own.

The choices made by others affect you, while your choices affect them. You are not on a solitary pilgrimage. It is as if we are linked by invisible bonds, so that when one person decides to set out in a particular direction, that impacts everyone else, and especially those who are close by. Yet each single choice is personal and can be terrifyingly lonely—and perhaps painful to those we love. While we may postpone choices we know we should make, that itself is a choice and has its impact somewhere. We may procrastinate, but we still experience an inner obligation to take responsibility for our own truth and freedom.

The Ignatian Approach

We mentioned the *Spiritual Exercises of St. Ignatius* already and said that we would return to them. The *Exercises* are simple but profound: they help a person find God but also uncover our disordered tendencies, which warp our decision-making. Whereas our tendency is to put ourselves first and decide from the vantage point of what *we want*, Ignatius helps us become God-centred in our choices.

Ignatius was a keen observer of how human beings go about things. After his conversion at the age of thirty, he became anxious to please God by making right decisions about his life. "What ought I do for Christ?" he wondered. He thought of doing "great deeds" for Jesus, his new-found Lord and Master. But how? Should he become a hermit, or imitate the excesses of the saints of old, or go to live in the Holy Land, or whatever? Even when he settled on the basic idea of "helping others" rather than living out a solitary life, he still had to work out how to do this, especially with the Inquisition hovering around. Decision after decision followed, often worked out with great difficulty, but always with God in mind. He became a pilgrim, then a student of theology to assure his orthodoxy, then a gatherer of like-minded companions, then a priest, and finally a founder and leader of a religious order, the Jesuits. He spent the rest of his life making decisions about how to respond to the endless calls on his limited manpower. On his knees he shaped the *Constitutions of the Society of Jesus,* endlessly checking out what might be more to God's honour and glory. He wrote more than 7,000 letters that reveal his way of approaching all sorts of issues, whether it was a shortage of funds, a threatened invasion by the Turks, or a papal request to send men to some distant part of the world.

The *Exercises* are more a recipe-book for one's spiritual guide than a book for personal reading. In skilled hands they can bring about profound inner change and a Godward orientation of a person's life. The book has been named among those that have changed the world, and it continues to do so, but unobtrusively. It is full of hints about "discernment"—the sifting of motivations and influences that play on the heart. The material is too rich to be dealt with here, so we will simply introduce the topic and emphasise that God can be found in making your choices. I hope to elaborate on this topic in another book. Here I can only hint at the terrain to be covered.

Keys to the Process

New levels of trust in God are demanded when you try to make a decision with God's help. We *never know* as we make a choice—about a marriage partner, or a change of job, for example—how things will work out. Choices are made in good faith, but God stays with us all the way through, working to bring good out of the choice whether it was a good or a bad one. We decide; then God says, "Right! Now, how can we bring good out of that choice?" God likes us to exercise our freedom!

The image of an orchestra can help. All the musicians play their pieces: it is the composer and the talented conductor whose genius makes a symphony of the medley of sound. Likewise, God orchestrates the "music" of each of our life-choices into infinite harmony. But our music is not written out for us beforehand: we are free to create it as we go along. No doubt God can weave the off-key and discordant notes into the divine symphony, but we know not how. It is better, however, when we make decisions that are in harmony with God's desire, so far as we can know them. The following points are important to keep in mind when moving to a decision:

- God desires only what is best for us and wants us to be happy by becoming our true selves.

- God is intensely involved in decisions that affect the world and humankind but is also interested in the small decisions that shape individual lives.

- God puts good desires in us so that we will make wise and loving choices.

- Conscience is given us to guide us, as are the Gospels and the life of Jesus, and the whole Christian tradition.

- God prompts us interiorly all the time. We noted above Ignatius's conviction that God can deal directly with us, if we only attend.

- We can create difficulty for God. Ignatius speaks of himself as being "nothing but an obstacle" by impeding and undoing the Lord's work. Our "shadow side" has to be brought to the light, which involves plenty of inner work.

- God has a broad agenda for us: "Do good!" "Love one another!" "Forgive!" "Share with the poor!" "Do not be afraid!" "Take up your cross!" God, however, does not have a hidden blueprint for the world! We "find the will of God" by doing the best we can in our decision making. Creation is an ongoing and open process.

- God is pleased with conscientious decisions. And we experience a sense of peace and harmony with God when this happens, even if the decision makes demands on us.

Freedom and Responsibility

The *Spiritual Exercises* are all about choices and how to make them well. Ignatius is trying to educate people to make decisions, both big and small, along the patterns of Jesus' decision making. Ignatius believes that each individual decision is important because it affects the world. He is prepared, therefore, to spend much time helping people understand that the divine gift of their freedom can be put to the service of God's project for the good of humankind.

Ignatius requires that we face the waywardness and disorder of our own freedom, but he encourages us to believe that a purified freedom is the best gift we can offer to God. Thus, the two freedoms, God's and ours, can work harmoniously together. The image of two lovers, each responding to and evoking the best in the other, catches the point.

Ignatius invites us to contemplate the life of Jesus, so that we can make decisions from within the same perspective he did. Just as Jesus tried to please the Father in all his choices, so Ignatius proposes that the love which moves me to choose between options "should descend from above"—that is, from God.

SUGGESTED EXERCISE

- When you are next alone with Jesus, you might ask him how he felt when he knew he had to make the decision about leaving Nazareth. Life was now going to be different; his future was uncertain; his only certainty was his trust in his Father's love.

- "How was it for you, Jesus? Were you lonely, uncertain, afraid? You knew you would be different. Did you perhaps not like that feeling? Did you think that others would be uncomfortable with your being different?"

- "How did you come to terms with the heartbreak of leaving your mother, whom you loved so dearly? Having made your choice, how much were you able to share with her about your dream? You must have known that her life and her relationships would be affected by your choice."

- You might chat with Jesus along these lines, and perhaps also speak with Mary, asking how she came to terms with her son's decision. Perhaps the three of you can chat together.

CHAPTER 13

A Labouring God

What Does God Do All Day?

Ignatian spirituality is *incarnational*. Incarnational spirituality infers a willingness to be involved with humankind in all its struggles, whereas disincarnate spirituality wants to remain safe, distant, and unengaged. The spirituality of Jesus was incarnational from the moment the three divine Persons agreed on the means of the world's salvation. Earth is home for God. God can say, "I love this place; this is where my son used to live!"

God, says Ignatius, *works and labours* on our behalf in all created things on the face of the earth. Among created things he lists "the heavens, elements, plants, fruits, cattle, etc. He gives them being, conserves life, gives growth and sensation." This is an explosive assertion! It means that from now on I can look on *everything* as touched by divine hands. God is there, everywhere, and I can find him. When I see things thus, I walk a transfigured world. I can also find God in the reality of labour itself. God is acting through those who labour, and God is active in all my labour. Ours is a labouring world—we can understand this word in a variety of ways. It can mean giving birth as well as involvement in grinding tasks. God is labouring through me even as I try to express my little insights at this moment. "Labouring" has also an overtone of toil and suffering. Jesus laboured and toiled to spread the good news of the Kingdom of God in the face of opposition, and in a sense he does so still, because he works with us who are his body. Can I, mysteriously, in my weariness and frustration, find God?

Responding to Conflict

Ignatius invites us to focus continually on the person of Jesus and to follow his way; he is the one who becomes fully human, who lives, walks, and talks with companions, prays, feels love and friendship, becomes angry, cries, puzzles over choices, and, like each of us, is affected by other people's choices. Good and just relationships mean everything to him, and he is constantly challenging us to become more loving with one another and with God. By living out our lives with our gaze on him, we can find God in all we do.

Jesus' world, like our own, was full of conflict. How did he conduct himself in it? He made endless choices as he faced each successive situation. The Gospels are about choices, stances, attitudes. He comes across as someone who has hope for everyone. He sees and affirms the hidden potential in the worst of people, the "sinners" who come flocking to him as their only hope. Because he believes in them, they come to believe in themselves. He has space for literally everyone.

He is not against anyone, but he challenges those who have illusions about themselves to become aware of their falsehood and self-deception. Knowing the truth, he promises, can set them free (John 8:32). He works for the radical cure of the human heart rather than glossing over our inner sickness. He labours to purify and liberate the human spirit. He entices us to desire the fullness of life, the life of glory.

When people reject and persecute him, he doesn't become embittered and hardened against them. Instead, he reveals a reserve of forgiving love, which may eventually melt the most stubborn hearts.

In this patient enduring of what is done to him, he reveals the fullness of love. This love is limitless; it bursts all boundaries, and it can transform the impoverished relationships that spoil our lives.

Stepping Out

Why did Jesus leave Nazareth to begin a new life as an itinerant preacher? Why did he not remain in safe obscurity, living a hermit's life and saving the world by interceding for it? His life-choice must have involved long heart-searching. If during his public ministry he frequently took time out of busy days to pray, he must have done likewise in Nazareth.

During those years, he must have grown in awareness of the depth of people's need for the Good News. He had the options of helping them at a distance or engaging in their lives so that they would become changed from within. Surely, he asked his Father, "What ought I do?" He wanted to share the treasure he held, namely that God is extravagantly in love with humankind. But how would he be received? Who would look after his mother if he left home? His was a hard choice, but we can guess that he experienced it as emerging from an insistent need to be authentic and to respond to the drawing of his Father.

As his decision unfolds, we watch Jesus face a variety of options. The temptations reveal his struggle to choose always to put his Father first. Later he must have wondered whom to choose as apostles. In his agony we see him facing a free but terrible choice. When we contemplate him on the cross, we can ask whether his freedom has now been totally taken from him. But we come to see that, even when completely trapped and nailed down, he is choosing to accept patiently and lovingly a situation he cannot change. This is where he wants to be, revealing God's heart as broken open in love for us. In our decision making we can be strengthened by watching the Son of God labouring to choose what would be best.

Suffering Can Be Redeemed

Like Jesus, we have choices we can make freely. There are other situations when, like him, all we can do is choose how to endure. How can we find God in situations such as sickness and death, from which we cannot escape? We can do so by choosing the right attitude toward them. Suffering that can't be avoided can still be redeemed. On Calvary, while one criminal was screaming at Jesus to save himself and them, the second rebuked him and begged help from Jesus, whom he saw to be innocent. This man's suffering, though he had brought it on himself, was redemptive. It was the occasion of his conversion of heart.

When we focus on Jesus, the innocent one, we find that his attitude towards his betrayal, torture, and death was one of patient acceptance, in forgiveness and love. He could only have hoped that this attitude would be pleasing to his Father, and it was. It brought about the radical redemption of humankind. We know this from the Resurrection: in raising Christ from the dead, the Father has gone guarantor that his Son's free decision to accept patiently what was being done to him is the divinely chosen way to break the vicious cycle of human evil. The Resurrection is the enduring proof that love is the only right response to hate, that patience and kindness will soften human hearts. Christian spirituality, contemplating Calvary, came to speak of *the law or dynamic of the Cross*. Simply put, it says that unavoidable suffering, patiently endured, is redemptive. Each of us endures a great deal: we are vulnerable and mortal. To know that we can find God even in the passive dimensions of our existence is a great encouragement in dark times. Suffering can indeed be a trap that breaks the human spirit, but it can also be an opening into a world of greater love.

Hope for the World

Since, as we have seen, God can be found in every choice we make, there is hope for our world. At the most radical level the world is in good hands because God has chosen to love it. It is indeed disfigured, a vandalised masterpiece, but through the work and example of Jesus its restoration is under way. Restoration is a slow process, requiring great expertise and endless patience, and it is costly. I know something of this because I live in the Jesuit residence in Dublin where *The Taking of Christ* by Caravaggio was discovered in the 1980s. It had hung in the dining room for fifty years, perfectly disguised by layers of dirty varnish and because it carried the signature of another painter. All the overlays had to be removed, centimetre by centimetre, without damaging the original.

This helps me; the painting becomes an image of the restoration of the world, which is primarily in divine hands and so is irrevocably underway. But, wisely or unwisely, God invites each of us to help in this delicate work, so Ignatius invites us to become sensitive crafters, tentative and open to divine directives. If we sometimes wonder "What does God do all day?" we now know! God is busy coordinating us for the restoration of the world. But we can also imagine the Trinity murmuring to one another, "It's pretty hard to get good staff these days!" So, while they remain undaunted by the difficulties and resistances we can place in their way, it helps if we ask to be educated and formed in the preferred way the Trinity like to go about things.

Realistic and Hopeful

Ignatian spirituality offers us the divine perspective on the world. It is both realistic and hopeful. It appeals for our engagement, especially through the making of wise choices. Although we can feel daunted in the face of the anti-human forces that dominate our world, God empowers us to make those difficult choices which may be required to advance God's project. Ignatius warns us that life can indeed be demanding: undisturbed enjoyment of divine company and human happiness is for a future time! But while the world is full of famines and disasters, murders, violence, and terrorism, it is also full of surprises and goodness. Awe, wonder, reverence, and excitement should characterise us because the deep-down mystery of the world is that God loves it infinitely, and we can come to see this more and more.

SUGGESTED EXERCISE

- By now you will be used to spending some time sitting or walking and talking with Jesus.
- Recalling what you have just read, and speaking exactly as one friend speaks to another, you might ask Jesus how it felt to walk the journey to Calvary. Allow Jesus to respond.
- "What was going on in your heart as you struggled along and felt the hostility of the people you loved?"
- "Were you in shock at the fact that your life was ending like this, when all you had ever done was to go around doing good?"
- "Death on a cross—Why? You had spoken of love and good relationships. How could it all go so sour?"
- "Was it a terrible struggle for you to choose not to be bitter or hard or condemnatory?"
- "Dear Jesus, I struggle like you with the pain of betrayal and broken dreams. Help me have your attitude of heart. Help me believe that my suffering can be worthwhile."
- Bring your prayer to a close by asking Jesus' blessing on yourself and your world.

CHAPTER 14

Companions of Jesus

While Ignatius believed deeply in the value of each person, he was in no way individualistic in his search for God and God's greater service. He kept his eye on how Jesus went about things. Jesus, more than anyone else in human history, gets fully involved with God and with the world. But he does not work alone. He gathers disciples and forms them into a band around himself. They are to be with him but also to be sent out, and he sends them off in pairs rather than alone. Ignatius wanted to do the same: he thought of orchestrating a small band of companions who would work together in pairs or larger numbers. If they were to be scattered across the face of the known world of his time, they were to be bonded together in union of minds and hearts.

Here we look at what it means to be a companion of Jesus, and what is entailed in living in companionship with others.

Personal Relationship

Ignatius keeps pointing to Jesus, never to himself. He is much more interested in facilitating our relationship with Jesus than in constructing an abstract theory of spirituality.

It has been said that his genius lay in his capacity to attract people who had strong desires and a high level of imagination—people who could see things in colour rather than in black and white, people who were not confined to one- or two-dimensional living.

Ignatius suggests all kinds of helpful ways to enable such people to focus on the Jesus of the Gospels. The process initiates a transformation. Those who practise imaginative contemplation of the Gospel scenes find themselves won over to Jesus, not only on the level of intellect and will but also on the levels of imagination, affectivity, feelings, and emotions. Quite simply, a falling in love goes on: deep engagement leads to intimate appreciation of Jesus, so that his vision and values and attitudes are assimilated. Recall the reflection attributed to Pedro Arrupe at the beginning of this book: falling in love changes everything and you begin to find God all around you. Your behaviour gains a new focus, which "decides everything."

Ignatius, in other words, has a special gift to help people identify with the mind and heart of Jesus, so that for the rest of their lives they will want their choices to coincide with the desires of God. He believes that if we watch carefully and lovingly the life of God-become-human, we will know how to live. Ignatian spirituality fosters Christian discipleship, and that is why it is found to be so helpful to an incredible variety of people, in fact to anyone trying to live out a Christian life.

Companions of Jesus

It becomes clear from the above why Ignatius insisted that the name of his little group must be "Companions of Jesus." This of course is not a description reserved for Jesuits. It is open to all who identify with the values of Jesus, who support one another and work out by discernment what God may want them to do. Many persons live out Ignatian spirituality "informally" in ordinary life; others group together in various ways, as in the Christian Life Communities.

The word *companions* literally means a group who break bread together: *panis* is the Latin for "bread"; *com-pan* means sharing bread. The first Jesuits saw themselves, in Ignatius's words, as "friends in the Lord." For each of them, their relationship with Jesus was primary, and this love made it easy for them to love one another, and it inspired everything they did. Like them, we can "break bread" with Jesus and with one another, and deliberate with his help how we can best bring his love to a needy world.

The term "friends in the Lord" offers a parallel and rich image of association. It is good to know that from Ignatius's time it refers not only to Jesuits but to those who bond with them through Ignatian spirituality. United in love of the Lord, we become friends with one another. Together we can find God more easily than when alone.

Into Our World

The goal of Ignatian spirituality, as we have said before, is to find God in all things. Before the Incarnation, people were surely justified in thinking that God, the Holy One, could be found only beyond this world. God was therefore considered distant, inaccessible, keeping the divine hands clean from the messiness of human situations. God was also understood to be a single Person: "God is One."

But with the Incarnation things changed dramatically. First, the place where God wishes to be found is here! We don't have to look up to heaven to find God but to look around us: distance has disappeared, and God is immediately present, as close to us as our neighbours. The treasure, the pearl of great price, is not hidden in some distant place but in ourselves and in the person next to us. Everything about our lives is God-touched and important. The human and divine are meant to be as inseparable in us as they are in Jesus. Each of us may be frail and wayward, but we are God-touched and so are of infinite dignity.

Since God has become human, we can encounter him in every-thing that is human—all points of interaction between human beings have now become privileged meeting places with God. Every place, no matter how unlikely, where we find human beings, is a holy place: hospitals for instance, where people are born and healed and suffer and also die; waiting places, whether nursing homes, prisons, refugee camps, bus stops, unemployment lines or lines to the confessional; tables for meals and meetings, and human celebrations.

Furthermore, God is involved in all relationships, not as a polite observer but creatively and warmly: whatever is good and constructive in the relationship is the work of God's grace. We find him in friend-ship, in marriage with its loyalty, fidelity, and durability, which are most evident in times of stress. And, insofar as genuine love exists in any relationship, even though it may not conform to established norms, God is involved.

The second surprise is that Jesus is the Son of God, so now there are two divine Persons! And slowly the Christian community came to see that there is a third, the Holy Spirit. This all seems impos-sible, but there it is. The God of Surprises indeed! Since, however, God is "social," God creates us as social. God loves community and interrelatedness. This has all sorts of implications for human living. But those who live out of Ignatian spirituality are helped if they link together in their following of Jesus. Jesuits are not always the best examples of this. They have often been accused of rugged individ-ualism—not surprisingly, because they are often involved in solitary work. This is why Ignatius insisted on strong relationships among his companions, and recently the Jesuits have been invited to see com-munity itself as witnessing to the Kingdom of God. If we are to proclaim the dignity of persons, a first step is to associate on a level of equality with others. Communities, however small or transient, are a privileged place where God is to be found, because God is a social God and the divine Persons live in loving relationships.

The Extravagant Lover

You probably know the prayer commonly attributed to Ignatius:

> Dear Lord, teach me to be generous,
> to give and not to count the cost,
> to fight and not to heed the wounds;
> to toil and not to seek for rest,
> to labour and to ask for no reward
> save that of knowing that I do your holy will.

There is no evidence that Ignatius composed this prayer, and, taken out of context, it can be harmful. It can suggest a grinding service in which I do all the giving. The question arises: Why should I "do the holy will of God" in the demanding ways suggested by this prayer?

Quite simply, companionship with Jesus begins from a different place, though it ends with the sentiments of this prayer. Companionship flows from falling in love with the Son of God *because he has first loved me*. I become aware that God, as an extravagantly generous lover, gives everything to me, his sometimes wayward beloved. Overwhelmed with gratitude, I want to respond generously and out of love. But the manner of my responding must not be dictated by some heroic decisions of my own making. Instead, I must try to be sensitive to what God invites me to do, and to that I say a loving "Yes." For Ignatius, God always leads. Our goal, then, is not to strike out on our own but to follow Jesus. He will always give us "the love and the grace" required to respond rightly to what he asks.

SUGGESTED EXERCISE

- See Jesus at a distance coming towards you. He holds out his hand as you approach each other. Perhaps he is a little breathless as he moves to greet you: he is eager and smiling, and you feel that he is happy to meet you.
- Feel the warmth and strength of his hand clasped in your own.
- As you walk or sit with him, can you risk telling him how you feel about him?
- The phrase "I simply love you" plays in the air like music. Can you say it? If you do, what happens in him? Do his eyes change, does he smile or clasp your hand again?
- How does he respond?
- Spend some time in letting this intimate encounter develop.
- Remind yourself often during the day that you are the companion of Jesus. Notice things change!

CHAPTER 15

How to Listen to God

An early biographer of Ignatius, Jeronimo Nadal, emphasised that Ignatius "followed the Spirit that led him; he did not go before the Spirit." (See Brian Grogan, *Alone and on Foot*, An abridgement of *Solo y a pie* by Tellechea Idigoras. Dublin: Veritas, 2008, 212.) He had the ability to listen attentively to an inner Presence deep within his being. He was a perpetual, sensitive listener to the word of God.

Inner Presence

Can we become like that? Is it possible for us to learn from Ignatius how to become ever more sensitive to the "inner Presence" deep within our beings, and so to find him in the depth of our hearts? The answer is a very definite "Yes." Ignatius himself encourages us and offers helpful guidelines on how to listen to what is going on inside us so that we can more easily find our way forward and make our choices well.

At first, we may catch on only occasionally to the fact that God is present for us, helping and guiding us. But with practice, we can remember more spontaneously and turn "to listen attentively and carefully to an inner Presence deep within."

Ignatius was not in communication with God only during prayer and when offering Mass, but he also grew steadily in his capacity to find God in all things. We have noted that shortly before he died in his mid-sixties, he acknowledged that whenever he wished, at whatever hour, he could find God. We, too, can become more sensitive to God as a cherished life-companion who shares every detail of our lives.

I Am Never Alone

I can come to a deep awareness that the Holy Spirit is *for me*, personally and uniquely, that the Spirit is aware of my particular situation and where I am right now. I don't have to be in the "correct place" in order to meet with the Holy Spirit. I don't have to reach some exalted level of holiness before being addressed by the Spirit. No, the Holy Spirit is glad to be with me, in my present situation. The Spirit wouldn't prefer to be with someone more interesting or important but just wants to be with me, to encourage me, to prompt me, and to draw me to what is good.

"You have made us for yourself, and our hearts are restless until they rest in you," St. Augustine said, but we misunderstand him if we think he meant that our hearts will remain restless until we meet God at the end of our lives. In fact, our hearts can rest in God throughout our lives. At this very moment, even as you read this, you can be resting in God and believing that God gazes on you and smiles. Try it! Trust your inner experience: it is God-given.

Can you trust enough to believe that God smiles on you? That God is both realistic and hopeful about you, as we said earlier? It is easier to believe that God shakes his head in disappointment when we get it all wrong. But the reality is that, while God is sad for our very real difficulties, he never, never gives up on us. Divine hands are always outstretched, gently encouraging us to try again.

If someone asked you for another word for "God," you could offer the phrase "Loving Presence," for that is what God is. When Moses asked Yahweh his name, Yahweh replied, "I am who I am," and this means "I am present. I shall be there *for you*." God is intimately present to everything, but especially to us. God's name is Emmanuel, which means "God is *with us*." Matthew's Gospel ends with the marvellous statement: "Know that I am *with you* always; yes, to the end of time." One way that promise is fulfilled is in the sacraments. Through them Christ chooses to make himself present to us across space and time. It is Christ who baptises, Christ who forgives, Christ who attends at the bedside of the sick. We meet him in all the important moments of our lives, under various simple forms: bread and wine, water and oil, gestures of blessing, words of healing. We meet God directly in the sacraments.

Recognising His Presence

The following testimony is a good example of how we can grow in this sort of awareness.

My daughter was ill for eight years when she was a child. My prayer was constant and desperate: "Make my little girl better—Now!" I believed that God would be there for my daughter, but I had no sense at the time that God was there *for me*. I couldn't catch on to the ways in which he was trying to show himself to me, even through her illness. He was offering me something good, but I was fixated on one thing—an immediate miracle.

Only slowly did I catch on to certain values, which I would have missed if I hadn't been in that situation. For instance, illness was considered shameful in our family. But through meeting other people with similar problems I came to accept that illness is part of life. In waiting rooms and clinics, as parents shared their troubles, supported each other through difficult times, and rejoiced when the news was good, I learned the true value of people.

I now see that God was intensely present to me and involved, but I had no awareness that I could have leaned on him and asked him to put his arm around me while my daughter was enduring those terrible tests. But now he and I sit together in waiting rooms and at the ends of beds: mothers wait a lot, but they need not wait alone.

"You were with me but I was not with you." This was Augustine's conclusion as he reflected over his sinful years: God was with him even then, in his sinning, but he had distanced himself from God, and perhaps that was more damaging than his sexual waywardness. Notice that Augustine in his *Confessions* addresses God directly: "You and I." If during his wayward years he could have spoken with God about his problems, things would have been different for him. When we sin, we must try immediately to get back into conversation with God, to restore the relationship we have broken off, and to work with a helping God through the problem we have created.

Consolation

If God is totally present to us, can we in turn be present to God, aware of God, focused on God? Surely, yes: God is a self-revealing God, who wants us to know he is there for us and wants us to catch on to his presence. Ignatian spirituality helps us, as we have seen, to become aware of God's presence. The more this awareness grows, the easier it is for us to find God. But what are the tell-tale signs that God is around?

Ignatius uses the term *consolation* to indicate the inner experience of being turned toward God, while *desolation* refers to the experience of being turned away from God. The terms describe the contrary orientations of the human spirit. Both are accompanied by feelings and emotions that alert us to them. When we catch on to what is happening, we have to make a decision: "Shall I go with this or not?" So the terms are tightly packed, because they involve the whole person. Ignatius tries to describe them as he convalesced in Loyola after breaking his leg at Pamplona. Daydreaming about his ladylove gave him joy, but it was transient. Dreaming about the lives of Christ and the saints also gave him joy, *but it remained steady.* Slowly he noticed what was going on in the alternating experiences: one course of action would be in tune with his deepest self, and the other would be out of sync with it. Slowly he came to his life-decision: he would follow Christ. He believed that the Holy Spirit was leading and enlightening him to make this choice, while there were other influences working against this guidance and illumination.

Thus, for generously minded younger people, an experience of living with the destitute can bring an unexpected joy. But then the question arises, "Do I want to do this again, perhaps even for a longer period? But what about my career prospects?" Likewise, a married man may get briefly involved with another woman. The experience brings a sense of freshness to his emotional and sexual life. But there is shame, too. What choice to make?

Consolation can be described in many ways. It is a sense of harmony, peace, appropriateness, authenticity. I may say, "I'm together." Energy is focused on what is good and loving. Strength and courage are present and a feeling of being able to cope, even though a decision may bring difficulty: "I'm facing the right way now." There is a sense of being in the light rather than in the dark about the way forward.

Such are some of the indicators of God's presence, and we can be alert to them. Consolation may carry a good mood, but deeper down it is a conviction. When you land in prison for protesting an injustice, you might feel a sense of elation at first. But thirty days on, that mood has long gone, yet your conviction of having done the right thing sustains you still.

Try to identify moments that bring a smile or a sense of peace: you will interpret them rightly as moments of consolation. Be aware of them as "God-moments," for they carry the touch of God, the smile of God, the nod of God's gratitude or approval. When Ignatius said he could not live without consolation, he meant not a heady mood but a conviction that he was doing the right thing, that he was God-oriented, even if in pain and distress.

Desolation

Contrary to consolation is desolation. It is as if the light has gone out and you are left in the dark. You sense that God is absent. You are out of sorts, off-key or off-centre; you are in a spin, fragmented and moody, preoccupied with inner struggles, missing out on joy, seeing things as grey or black. You feel unsure, unhappy, separated, and lonely. You lose courage. It is hard to be loving and kind and easy to put bad interpretations on everything. Your judgements can be quite unbalanced and negative. Clearly, in desolation your demons are hard at work, whereas in consolation your good spirit is leading.

Notice that it is easier to describe desolation than consolation! When we are in our dark moods, we think we *are* darkness: we identify ourselves with it. "I am bad, useless, out of place, I feel rotten about myself." It would help so much if we could distinguish ourselves from our mood. The next time you feel desolate, try saying the following: "I have a bad mood. I, who am good, have a bad mood. But it will pass, and I will come back to my true self soon. I am in the dark now, but the light will soon shine again."

Walking in the Light

God wants us to be in consolation, not in desolation nor in some grey area in between. The glory of God is the human person fully alive, as St. Irenaeus said 1800 years ago. We are made for God, and when we are faced towards God, we are in consolation. We are in the light, in tune with God, on track, in the right place, no matter how we happen to feel. At the end of his prayer in the Garden, Jesus was at peace at the deepest level of his being. He was in consolation, even though he was distressed on all levels of emotion and feeling. Thus, both consolation and desolation, each in its own way, can help us in our search for God.

Consolation can be present as much in the wintry times of our lives as in the bright periods. The wind that blows my boat into harbour can be cold and piercing—or a gentle breeze. Either will do. What matters is that I am on course and moving towards God. Peace and harmony can often be deep down, and I may need to search for them beneath surface turbulence. As someone said, "I have vowed to be celibate and believe it is right for me. But my hormones don't seem to hold the message!"

SUGGESTED EXERCISE

As you go about your day, chat along with Jesus. As events occur, share them with him.

- "Jesus, I'm going for this interview . . ."
- "I'm lying here alone and in pain. Nobody seems to care . . ."
- "Forgive me when my heart goes sour and I become mean and ungrateful . . ."
- "I'm looking forward to the big match . . ."
- "I'm going to feed the baby . . ."
- "Jesus, I'm stuck. I don't know what to do . . ."
- "Thank you for the wonderful surprise you gave me today!"

Thus, you meet the Lord moment by moment. He is there for you, in intimate companionship.

CHAPTER 16

Like a Falling Tear

As a follow-up to the last chapter, it will help to elaborate briefly on Ignatius's idea of discernment. Imagine a pilot of a plane or ship peering into the mist to see the way ahead; there you have a simple image of discernment. The pilot needs to see through the mist to find his way safely. Another image of discernment, used in the early days of the Church, was of money changers distinguishing good coins from counterfeit ones. They could sift through a heap of coins, with a quick and accurate eye for the good and the bad. Their livelihood depended on "getting it right."

What Is Discernment?

The gift of discernment is the capacity to distinguish the good from the bad, especially when the bad is dressed up under the appearance of good. The discerning heart can also distinguish between two good options. "Shall I give a large sum of money to my son for his studies, or instead share it with the destitute?" Because Ignatian spirituality is centred on finding God through the making of good decisions, discernment is central to it. Different options can seem both good and attractive: how can we know which of them has God's approval in this particular situation?

Ignatius offers guidelines to help us discern our way forward, and these come from his reflection on personal inner experience. In the last chapter, we looked at consolation and desolation, and you were invited to notice these inner states, these feelings and moods, in your own experience.

Do you notice times and situations and choices that carry with them a sense of energy, peace, and joy? Is there a movement forward in the way of true love? Perhaps you spent time with a sick person, even though you had many other things to do. Or perhaps you were feeling sorry for yourself and, having wallowed in your misery for a while, you turned to God and begged for help and found yourself stronger and freer as a result.

Sense of Direction

Since we are made for God, turning to God will always bring consolation—that is, strength, peace, courage, togetherness. For when we move towards God, we are "on our thread," "on the right wavelength."

We are a bit like homing pigeons! Disoriented when released from their cages hundreds of miles from home, they will circle for a while and then unerringly find their true direction and follow it through thick and thin until they land, perhaps exhausted, in their own coop!

Just as something deep within assures the birds that they are on the right path, so in us the experience of consolation assures us that we are moving in God's direction or, more simply, in the direction of love.

Spiritual Consolation

As an aside, it is important to note that by consolation Ignatius always means spiritual consolation, the consolation of the Good and Holy Spirit of God. There are other consolations: that of the addict getting another "fix" or that of the bank robber who gets away with a big haul. Their feelings of joy or excitement are not from God. These feelings mask inner unhappiness, which soon returns.

This fact brings us to yet another insight about ourselves and how we can find our way more securely: the experience of desolation can be helpful insofar as it makes us realise that we are going the wrong way. It is saying, "Wrong Way! Go Back!" On motorways, such signs are frightening but helpful: they save lives.

Through Darkness to Light

Here's an example of how desolation can befriend us. An authoritarian priest was asked by some parishioners to meet with them. The meeting was a heated one: the honest anger of the parishioners disconcerted the priest, who went off feeling shattered and depressed.

Days passed. At times he felt like punishing the people and asserting himself as "The Boss." At other times their final words at the meeting played on his heart: "We love you, Father, and we respect you for all you do for us. But we want our needs to be taken into account." "We love you . . ." And they showed it by their gentle sensitivity while he struggled in his valley of darkness.

Finally he yielded to the Good Spirit, and in a homily that was both painful and joyous, he told what had happened and proposed a meeting—to be chaired by a laywoman!—on how he and the parishioners might work together as a parish.

Thus, desolation can be a pathway to true consolation. Never ignore desolation: it is trying to tell you something you need to know, just as physical pain does.

Discerning Hearts

I suggest that we all have such experiences as the dominating pastor. Contrary influences "stir" us, and it is a great help to us if we reflect on them and see where each is leading. Thus, we become persons of discerning hearts, which is what Paul asked for the Philippians: "In my prayers I ask that your love may lead you each day to a deeper knowledge and clearer discernment, that you may have good criteria for everything. So you may be pure of heart and come blameless to the day of Christ" (Philippians 1:8–10). By "heart" we mean the centre within us from which our convictions flow.

In a delightful image, Ignatius contrasts the action of the good and bad spirits on a sincere heart. "The good spirit touches the soul gently, lightly, sweetly, like a drop of water falling on a sponge. The evil spirit touches it sharply, with noise and disturbance, like a drop of water falling on a stone." A drop of water, or a tear, is a tiny thing: try noticing how it falls differently on absorbent or hard surfaces—silent attention is demanded!

Similar attention is demanded to notice the action of the Good Spirit on your heart, but the reward is that you can move along securely in the ways of God and help others to do so too. God is constantly drawing you, tugging at your heart, quietly beckoning, working silently in all things for your good, and you can find him through attending to your own heart. Savour this wonderful mystery: your heart is a holy place where God and you can always meet!

Good and Evil

Let us return to the issue raised earlier: how to cope with wrongdoing and evil and the sad dimensions of human life. Especially when things are hard, we need constantly to be reminded that a good influence is at work in us, countering the negative and destructive influences that are all too obvious. We can feel small and helpless in the great conflict between what is good and what is anti-human and anti-divine, but the Holy Spirit is steadily present to us, helping us, and others through us, to realise our high destiny, which is to be the sons and daughters of God.

The Holy Spirit does not remove us from conflict to a safe place. Rather, the conflict is in us and around us, but the Spirit evokes the best in us and gives us, through consolation, the signs we need to stay close to and to act rightly with God, who labours to transform situations and structures that are de-humanising, ungraced, and ungodly.

How do we find God in what is bad or evil? While we can find God directly in the good that surrounds us, because God is its source, God's presence is more indirect in the dark dimensions of life, because God is **not** their source. We can then easily miss the remedial work of God. This work is often disguised, and it does not undo the damage done, and yet we can find the consoling touch of God's hand in evil, if we search carefully.

We think we would be consoled in bad situations if God were to eliminate evil-doers and restore things to where they were before things went wrong. But—at least since the Flood!—God does not work that way. The ways of human justice, of crime and punishment, are not God's preferred style. So where is God in the tragedies, scandals, outrages, and crimes that soil the pages of human history?

Christian thinking starts from and returns endlessly to the passion of Jesus in its effort to make sense of suffering. The betrayal, false condemnation, torture, and horrible death of an innocent man who was also the Son of God were bad in themselves. The Friday on which Jesus died should surely have been called "Black Friday," just as the slaughter of unarmed civil rights marchers in Derry in 1974 was called "Bloody Sunday." But instead, that Friday two thousand years ago is still called "Good Friday" because out of its darkness was revealed the limitless quality of the love which God has for humankind. The Father forgave us for the worst we could do against Jesus, his Son. The immense hatred and cruelty shown in what Jesus endured acted as a foil for the radiance of divine love, which reconciles humankind to God. Jesus' suffering, patiently and lovingly endured, gives birth to a new understanding of the forgiving mercy of God, which we could never have guessed otherwise. Desolation yields to consolation.

The Law of the Cross

From contemplating the passion, the Christian community came to see that *God is at work everywhere in human waywardness and evil to bring good out of it.* This is the characteristic work of God, and it is consoling. Thus, we can—at least sometimes—find God in bad situations. It is not that the clock is rolled back to the point before the evil began. No, the Passion remains as an enduring fact: Jesus did die, and the resurrected Jesus still bears his wounds. Likewise, an innocent girl bears the scar of rape for a lifetime. But sometimes we see a wronged person developing a maturity out of the battle to integrate an adversity. We see new dimensions of love unfold in a husband who cares for his wife who has dementia. We see moments of reconciliation, of conversion, and so on. Of course, such events are all too few, but they occur, and when you identify them, you are finding God. Only at the End will we see the weave God has made of all the wrongs begotten of erratic free will.

From another perspective, God is in solidarity with all victims. If one part of the body of Christ suffers, Jesus too suffers. The painful pilgrimage that is human history wends its way along, and the Cross is set on a vantage point that all can see, gaining strength from the conviction that God, against all the odds, cares for and supports each plodding figure. In this sense, the Cross acts as an appropriate vehicle by which Jesus shows his solidarity. Sensitive hearts such as that of Corrie Ten Boom, author of *The Hiding Place*, catch on to this solidarity and can teach us how God can seem to be doing nothing to resist human evil and cruelty, and yet the transformation of the sufferers is being achieved. We learn that God is helpless on one level: God will not revoke the gift of freewill from perpetrators, nor intervene miraculously to defend victims. Instead, God suffers with victims and works on their hearts to strengthen them and bring them a strange joy that does not come from their situation but from Godself. God also works in the hearts of good people so that they will do what they can to bring the cruelty to an end.

God is also present in evil by working to convert perpetrators from perversity of heart to goodness. The prompting of conscience reveals God at work. And in the final stage of life, when we seem to be falling apart, God is concealed as the One who hollows us out, so that we may be filled with Godself.

We Need Consolation

Ignatius spent the last phase of his life coordinating his newly founded Company of Jesus, making important decisions which were to transform the lives of many people across the world. The early Jesuits saw themselves as engaged in a ministry of consolation: they had learnt for themselves what consolation was like; they experienced it as the energy, purpose, and joy that came from being united with God in all they were trying to do, no matter how difficult the task or how daunting the opposition.

They must have echoed Ignatius's remark that "he could not live without consolation." What did he mean by that? Surely not constant euphoria and a feeling of being on top of the world! Rather, an inner conviction that what he was about, even if humble, painful, and laborious, was pleasing to God. Like Jesus, he asked no more and no less than this.

SUGGESTED EXERCISE

Today let us take the daily news for our exercise in finding God.

- As you pray in your quiet place, imagine an item or two from the news of the day. It may be a dramatic court case, a dreadful murder, an overturned ferry, a rumble of war far away, a report on refugees who have lost everything. Notice the effect on your heart and mood.

- Now see yourself walking towards Jesus as he stands alone on a little hill overlooking Jerusalem (Luke 19:41–44). Slowly, you become aware of the fact that he is weeping.

- Can you put your arm around his shoulder as he bows his head? Can you wipe his tears?

- You listen as he speaks about the hard-heartedness of the people he loves so much. They are preparing their own destruction. He says, "I'm tempted to turn away and distance myself from them. But instead I must call on Abba for new reserves of love."

- Then he turns to you and thanks you for being with him.

- He says, with a little smile: "From now on, why don't we watch or listen to the daily news together? We can pray together as the different items come up." Perhaps just say, "Lord, have mercy on us all."

- Tell him how that feels for you.

CHAPTER 17

Love Beyond All Telling

The central message of the Incarnation is that God is continually coming into our world because he loves us. He wants to be found. The birth of Jesus is a gentle event in one way but explosive in another: his coming turns everything inside out and upside down. Perhaps poets catch the point better than the rest of us: one of them, the Chilean Pablo Neruda, puts it thus:

> I searched for God in the heavens
> but found he had fallen to earth,
> so now I must search for him among my friends.

God is in our material world and in everything that is human. God's history and our history merge together through the Incarnation of the son of God. Our understanding of God, our world, and ourselves is transformed and illuminated. Ignatian spirituality is no more and no less than an effort to put words on this transformation.

All Things New

For Ignatius, everything was transformed in a basic way through an experience God gave to him at the Cardoner River near Manresa in 1522. The rest of his life was an unfolding of that radical experience. God revealed to him how he is present in all things; it was a mind-blowing experience that came out of the blue to this convalescent pilgrim as he was making his devotions. He later found it hard to talk about what had occurred, and yet years later when asked why he was deciding things in one way or another, he would reply, perhaps with a smile, "The explanation will be found in something that happened to me at Manresa." From his stumbling words we can gather the following: he was given a profound appreciation of the most Holy Trinity and of the Incarnation of the Son and how he is present in the Eucharist. Next, he says, "the manner in which God created the world was revealed to his understanding with great spiritual joy." Lastly, his mind was illuminated regarding "spiritual things and matters of faith and of learning." He notes that from this time on, *everything seemed new to him.*

It's All Extraordinary!

What would it be like for you if everything seemed new to you?

It's a puzzling question, isn't it? When Our Lady held her child in her arms, she must have had this sense of "everything seeming new" to her. God had broken into her life and become its Centre. Everything seems new when that happens: a God-event is what brings about the change. On the outside the world could look the same as before, but now that God has entered it, everything is fresh and surprising and bursting with new meaning. There's nothing boring about any aspect of human life. "The earth is charged with the grandeur of God," as G. M. Hopkins says. Humankind has been, as it were, "plugged into God": the divine current is energising every detail of human life from conception to death and into the fullness of eternal life. Because of the Incarnation, God can be sought and found in all human things. For this reason, ordinary affairs now matter infinitely because everything has a divine connection: all reality forms a seamless weave. Everything comes from God and can lead to God. We can never say this or that "has nothing to do with God." Nor can we say this or that "is boring," because God makes all things new.

As I write, I have some sense that there never was a day like today, even though I am engaged in the same task of writing, with the same computer, as I have been for quite a while. Instead, "This is the day the Lord has made. Let me be glad and rejoice in it." I like the Zen saying: "Every day a good day!"

Mary—Like Us?

Can we find the extraordinary hidden behind the ordinary in our own lives? Our Lady can help here. To her next-door neighbours in Nazareth Mary looked like a very ordinary mother, but something extraordinary was going on in her life. Our temptation is to think that she was extraordinarily graced and that the rest of us are not. But the truth is that while Mary has a unique and intimate relationship with God, God never intended it to create an unbridgeable distance between herself and us. The world is not divided between those who are highly favoured by God and those who are not! Mary would want to say to every mother, "Please don't distance me! Indeed, I am unique and have been specially graced, and my child is the chosen one of God. But you too are unique: you're specially graced, and your child is a chosen daughter or son of God also. Each of us is singled out for special loving attention by God and given what we need for our special role."

Ignatius describes his experience at Manresa as one in which *everything* seemed new to him. But the primary thing that was new was his *appreciation of himself.* Before the great change in his life, he thought of himself and was seen by others as a worldly man, obsessed with a desire for personal honour and glory. But now "it seemed to him that he was a different man and that he had a different intellect from the one he had before" (*Ignatius: Writings*, 27). Ignatius doesn't tell us exactly what the difference was, but was it perhaps that the blindness that hides from us our inner richness was removed from him? He seemed to see how close God was to him, how deeply God loved him, wanted him, gifted him. The door is open for us to enter a new world and become at home in it. We are, after all, divine family!

The Awakening

Ignatius had been graced with a breath-taking glimpse of the mystery of divinity within himself and also in all things human and in the material world. But the gift given to Ignatius is always being offered to you. God isn't hiding it from you. It is awaiting discovery, and the clues are scattered all around. Frail and limited though you be, you are in the process of becoming the daughter or son of God. The statue is on the block, and the sculptor is hard at work. Each detail of your life, good or bad, significant or otherwise, is being orchestrated by God. Everything that is good is being provided for you, while everything that is not good is being worked on by God and turned towards your lasting good. You are totally loved, and God is looking after you in every possible way, and so you can spend your life in seeking and finding God in everything. It is good to ask God to pull the veil back a little each day. Jesus knows that his Father wants to give us this gift. He says, "Ask! Search! Knock!" (see Luke 11:9–13). The divine response is promised: "Those who love me will keep my word, and my Father will love them, and we will come to them and make our home with them" (John 14:23).

Christmas encapsulates all that God has in store for us: God is fully present in one single human being but desires to be fully present in each one of us. Let it happen! Let the love that is beyond all telling find you and transform you!

SUGGESTED EXERCISE

- Jesus comes in, and after you have both settled down, he says, "We have been talking for the past while about finding God in everything. Now, today, if you have nothing special on your mind, let's look at how *gifted* you are."

- You smile in anticipation.

- He says, "First, let's review those gifts that are given to you alone. Shall we start with your very existence? God has had you in mind since the beginning of the world! You are uniquely an image of God, distinct from every other image. It's a bit like snowflakes—all of them distinct! Next, there are all your good qualities, your talents and skills, your intelligence, and your goodness of heart. Next, there is the fact that you have reached the age you are now. Providence has been on your side for that to happen: would you agree? Next, think of all the good that you bring to the world: you are a gift to others! And you have had many escorts of grace yourself, so let's list them—parents, family, friends, helpful people who make your life worthwhile . . ."

- You say, "Goodness me! How many I have taken for granted!"

- He smiles. "We're not done yet! Besides your unique gifts, there are the gifts you share with others—like the cosmos, and our planet, and the wonders of nature. Then there are all the resources that support your life. Think of yourself as gift-laden. God keeps the whole show going. Name anything good that is not a gift, if you can!"

- You respond, "I heard someone a while back saying, 'All is gift!' Now I'm beginning to see what she meant. And she had this beautiful look on her face as she said it . . ."

- He says, "There's more, of course, isn't there? You are the beloved of God. You are the focus of God's unwavering care. I have tried to show you this by coming into this world and dying for you so you can be with God forever . . ."

- You stammer, "I don't know what to say."

- "No need to say anything. I just wanted to help you move along in finding and loving God more and more. You can find God in yourself and in everyone and everything around you. God dwells here. God is always giving, loving, labouring, caring. Wherever you find these activities going on, you are stumbling upon God . . ."
- "Jesus, thank you. Please come back soon and remind me of all you've said just now. And please show me how to be a gift to others."

The Examen

Introduction

When I had completed a draft of this book, I invited a few friends to read it and come back with constructive criticisms. One of the readers said, "You've said nothing about the *examen*, but it's the best help I know in coming to find God in all things!" We talked about this and came to see that in fact the whole book is a lengthy *examen* because it touches on so many areas in which we can find God. But we also agreed that something helpful could be said on ways to go about the practice itself.

So, what is the *examen*? It comes from the Latin word for "examination" and has become a key word in Ignatian spirituality over the centuries. This is a short period of reflective prayer that focusses on the reality of your daily living. It will help you—as it does countless others—keep your life in tune with God's unfolding project for our world. No prayer is more characteristic of St. Ignatius of Loyola because it helps your life become an intimate partnership with God. The simplest image is of two friends, God and yourself, meeting for a cuppa and reviewing your day together. God has an agenda for you and for those you meet, so you want your ways of going about things to be in harmony with God's desires.

The *examen* or Review of Consciousness is not a logical analysis of your hours and days but a heart-to-heart affair, made not alone but with a loving and attentive God who is even more interested in your affairs than you are! With the help of this practice you begin to dance to God's music. You grow in your ability to be a companion of Jesus, who always tried to do what pleased his Father (John 8:29). We have spoken earlier about contemplation as being "a long, loving look at the real." The *examen* is a contemplative moment in which you take at least a *short* "loving look at the real." The "real" encompasses the bits and pieces and important matters that make up your day. You get accustomed to noticing the presence of God in the details of your life. For a few moments you take time out to see how God has been leading you, and you take direction from the good Spirit of God for the time ahead. Slowly you become made over to God.

There are many ways of making the *examen*, perhaps as many as the number of people who make it each day! It is highly adaptable. Here are a few examples, so that you can customise it for yourself. If you have more time, you can flesh out this reflective interlude further. Such an investment is always worthwhile. Socrates was right in asserting that the unexamined life is not worth living: the opposite is true also—my day truly comes to life when I take time with my God to savour the after-taste of my daily experiences. This is where the Spirit is at work: if an encounter with someone has left a good taste, the Good Spirit has had free play in my heart. If the encounter has left a sour taste, there is work to be done—perhaps I am being prompted to an apology or to a gentler style, or to face some awkward truth. "Sweet and sour" can serve as my rule of thumb for the worlds of consolation and desolation.

The Ten-Second Stop

I may be exhausted at the end of a busy day, so I tell God how I am feeling, and then say, *"Dear God, thanks for the good things you sent my way today!"* That's it, no more than a ten-second pause! But it is worthwhile to do even that. Why? Because I know God is close to me and supporting me. My little love call indicates a grateful heart, and in Ignatius's way of thinking, nothing is more important than gratitude.

Alternatively, I might imagine a blank sheet of paper. I write *"Dear God"* on the top, and at the bottom I write *"AMEN."* I then sign the page. The empty space can include random bits and pieces that strike me about the day: someone I met; a decision I made; things that happened to me; some hints of God's providence, like getting an encouraging smile from someone. I can include some feelings—feelings of consolation, energy, courage, despondency, anger, and so forth. I simply wrap the day up in the *"AMEN"* and send it off to God. I am saying in effect: *"Dear God, you have given me this day; here is what I have made of it. Bless me. Amen!"*

The Longer Pause

1. **"Hello!"**

   Since it is always good to meet with someone who loves me, I happily slow down to review the day with my God. Gradually mine becomes a **relational heart**.

2. **"Shine On Me!"**

   I ask God to walk gently back with me through the day and to give me light to see it as God sees it. Slowly I cultivate an **enlightened heart**.

3. **"Let's Explore!"**

God and I rummage through some of the day's events: my health; the weather; nature; what I did; who I met; what gladdened my heart or burdened it; my dominant feelings; nudges and challenges to grow in love; my prayer; decisions I made; the gentle touches of God's hand. Over time the grace of a **discerning heart** is given to me. I find God more easily, and that brings joy.

4. **"Thank You!"**

Everything good comes from God, so I thank God for blessing my day and for the good things I have done. Gradually I develop a **grateful heart**.

5. **"Forgive Me!"**

I may have been unkind or made a selfish decision. I ask God to heal anyone I have hurt or situations I have spoiled. Almost unnoticed, there is born in me a more **sensitive heart.** Those around me suffer less and can be more sure of me.

6. **"Bless Tomorrow!"**

I ask God to bless the time ahead. I want to be led by God in its particular challenges, because I am God's ambassador. Mine becomes a **hopeful heart** despite all difficulties and frustrations. God is with me, and I want to be with God in every one of my tomorrows!

Finding God in a New Age

A Spirituality of Decision Making

Decisions

Do you ever find yourself saying:

"My life seems to be in a rut, and I can't move forward."

"I'd love to be able to make good decisions consistently."

"Things just happen to me: I seem to have no personal power or responsibility."

"Life is too big for me. I'm not important, and I've no effect on what goes on."

"I do try to make right decisions, but how can I know that God is pleased with them?"

Inner peace, energy, and happiness depend on making good decisions. Ignatian spirituality helps people all over the world to make them well. *But what is Ignatian spirituality?*

Ignatius

St. Ignatius of Loyola (1491—1556) spent his life learning how to make good decisions in the fast-changing scene of the Reformation and the discovery of the New World. As one of the great "movers and shakers" of his time, his goal was to find God in all things. His influence has developed rather than lessened over the past 500 years, for he has much wisdom to offer as we search for God in the whirlwind of contemporary life.

Spirituality

Spirituality focuses on the *dynamic and concrete* character of your relationship to God in actual life situations. It concerns your *religious experience* rather than issues of faith or morality. Thus, Celtic Spirituality asks: "How did the Celts relate to God?" The Spirituality of Suffering asks: "How can I relate to God in what I am enduring?" Spirituality in a New Age asks: *"How can I relate my life to God in the 21st century?"*

You Are Important!

Ignatian spirituality helps you make dynamic connections among the three great realities that make up your life:

- Yourself
- Your world
- Your God

This is where good decision making is vital. Life is shaped by decisions. In making them, we must respect ourselves, the needs of our neighbour, and the intentions of our God. Then we can live out our lives fully and richly in the concrete. No decision we make is unimportant to God.

Do you believe that you—just as you are right now—are a remarkable person who has an extraordinary treasure within you? No matter how badly you may feel about yourself, you are limitlessly loved and special to God: "God doesn't do junk!" God has dreams for you. God respects your present reality and invites you to develop at your own pace, and Ignatian spirituality helps you take *your* next feasible step into an open world.

The insights of Ignatian spirituality are as follows:

- You're important to God and to God's world right now.
- You have unique gifts, imagination, and creativity.
- You have a special role to play in the drama of human history.
- God respects every decision you make, whether good or bad!

Ignatian spirituality is person-centred! Its focus is on *you*, rather than on saying prayers or performing devotions, good though these may be. It asks you instead: **"What are you doing with your life right now?"**

Direct Encounter

Ignatius maintains that God deals *directly* with you. He came to this realisation from his own inner experience. God draws you to what is true and good and loving, through your imagination, feelings, desires, needs, talents, and energy. God sets up events in your life, and you respond. Ignatius admits that God dealt with him like a school-teacher with a rather dull student. He slowly caught on to what God had in mind for him. He was 50 when he founded the Jesuits, and he died at 65! So, take yourself gently, but keep in touch with God, and let yourself be led. Ignatius was "Someone led by Another." It would be nice if that could be said of each of us.

God is active in all events and gives you the capacity to respond rightly to them. God waits, breathlessly and intently, as you move to your decisions. Even if you make a bad decision, God will respect it. God won't reverse a decision you make but will work to bring some new good out of it. Not easy! A 17-year-old became pregnant. She knew she couldn't manage to care for the child. Her partner proposed an abortion. No, that wouldn't be right, she felt. The partner left.

Her parents came to the rescue, at great personal cost, and reared the child. There are many decisions here. God prompts the good ones and wrestles with the bad ones. God looks out for help and engages good people to limit the damage of a bad choice. So, God gets us to carry one another along: You may find someone stepping in when you go wrong, and you in turn may come to the rescue of someone else. We get by together, with God's help.

Instead of thinking that God finished the work of creation quite some time ago, you are invited to think of God as creating all the time. You and everyone else are invited to partner with God in the work of creating the world of tomorrow.

Through reflective living you can become sensitive to the ways God touches your heart and inspires your mind. You can develop a discerning heart as you make your way along. You can be guided by the Good Spirit to find God more and more easily. There are no limits to the intimacy and creativity that can grow when two hearts are in harmony—yours and God's!

A Divine Companion

In the Gospels, we find Jesus gathering disciples: they were to be his life-companions. In his final conversation with them before his Passion, he emphasised that they were not his servants but *his friends*, and that the relationship which had grown between them and him was to continue even when he seemed absent. He promised that he would in fact always be with them, and he invited them to draw life and energy constantly from their relationship with him. This invitation is extended to us also today. We are to carry out our life tasks in companionship with Jesus. The friendship he offers is the same he offered his first companions. Friendship connotes heart-knowledge, which leads to intimate love and therefore to following.

This sense of companionship is the foundation of genuine Christian discernment. This means that I make my choices, not isolated and fearfully but in the company of Someone who cares deeply about what I do. This person will help me. I can turn to him in trust and say: "Let's work on this together!"

You can meet regularly with Jesus in the privacy of your heart. It also helps a lot at other times to meet him in company. The first disciples must often have forgotten that they had a divine companion to turn to. So they made mistakes. But when they gathered together, they would have started talking about Jesus and what he was like, what his values and vision were. They reminded one another of him, and so the Gospels got written! Each disciple had a unique relationship with Jesus, so when they shared this, they were given new heart and renewed vision. This got them back on track, like pilgrims on the Camino pilgrimage who gather in the evenings around a meal, talk about the day's journey done, and what route to take tomorrow. Pilgrims watch out for one another. This is what a "church" means: it is an assembly of like-minded people. The Christian Church is a group of disciples gathered around Jesus, their Leader. They sing, they talk, they share a meal. He, their Leader, provides the food and drink, his very self. They are given new heart and vision. They decide together about the way forward. This is what the Eucharist is about.

Serving Your World

Ignatian spirituality is a spirituality of *active service*. The forms of service are limitless, but they centre on the development of **good relationships between persons**. All reality is relational—so the scientists tell us—and we humans are meant to relate also. Our relationships are meant to mirror nothing less than the relationships among the Father, Son, and Holy Spirit. They get along very well together and are totally happy with each other! So, wherever we can improve relationships—at home, in the neighbourhood, the parish, the work-place, the UN—we are building up the kind of world God wishes for us all.

However, fostering good relationships in a broken world is a gigan-tic task. Think of genocides, world wars, greed, and domination by the powerful over the weaker. But healthy relationships remain the divine agenda! Always on Jesus' mind were love, forgiveness, respect, sharing, compassion. In short, he was **FOR** people and wanted people to be **FOR** one another! Through contemplative companionship with him, we catch on to his attitudes. "Contemplative companionship" means that I spend time watching Jesus lovingly. I look at the world with his eyes; I feel for people with his heart. This is what prayer should often be about: *taking a long, loving look, with Jesus, at the real-ity around me.*

Ignatius proposes that the Holy Spirit is close to us, deep in our hearts. Again, he stumbled on this fact by stopping to reflect on the inner nudges he experienced, which urged him in one direction or the opposite. We can notice this too. The Spirit nudges us steadily in the right direction so that we come to play our role well in God's world. When we are "on our thread," we experience peace, confidence, joy, authenticity, even though we might be taking on some demanding task, such as standing against injustice. When we're off track, we sense ourselves disturbed, unsure, fragmented, untrue to our best selves, and focussed inward rather than outward.

We believe that the Father, Son, and Spirit are intensely focussed on our world with all its problems; they are actively involved in it, and they look around the world in search of people who will be **FOR** others. Ignatius uses a homely image: *we are to be sensitive and pliable instruments in the divine hands.* Just imagine a surgeon whose instru-ments suddenly started doing their own thing in the middle of an operation! But that's what happens when we focus solely on ourselves.

If human history is a mess, it is because people decide that they want to "do it my way."

Divine Dreams

God's project for our world is an *open* one: it is anything but fixed and static. God is full of imagination: think of mice and giraffes, crocs and crocuses! God gets bored with mindless repetition. God's dream is more like the game-plan of a football coach than an architect's detailed plan for a house. A team tries to take into account all the variables created by the guile and craft of the opposition. The greater the depth of resources in the team, the better it can adapt to change. The openness of world process requires that often our decisions will have to be made in uncertainty and be frequently revised. But throughout our lives, we are to act *as wisely and lovingly as we can*. We are to believe, as Jesus did, that what is deepest and best in us is good enough for God. We are to stop regularly and ask God: "What will we do now?" In this way we become God's collaborators. God labours in our world, deciding to do what is wisest and best in every situation. We try to do likewise. The salvation of the world is a corporate event!

In Tune with Love

How do you see the world? Is it neatly ordered, with pre-arranged paths set down for each person? Or is it open—as open as the expanding universe of which our planet is a tiny part? How did Jesus view the world and his life in it? Did he see beforehand that suffering and death were his inevitable destiny? Or was he like us in all things, so that he found himself continually having to make choices? Was he often unsure, puzzled, confused, and even frightened? Did he experience regret, as we do, over decisions made in good faith but which did not work out, as in his choice of Judas?

In the Gospels we see a person trying to make choices that are appropriate to the emerging situations in which he finds himself. These situations often come about due to the conflict between his values and those of others. When Jesus says, "I always do what pleases him" (John 8:29), he does not mean that he simply does what the Father has planned for him. Rather, he means that in all the choices that confront him, he acts out of altruistic love and wisdom. While he must often have been perplexed and unsure, what keeps him going is his conviction that he must be busy, not with his own affairs but with his Father's. He believes that his Father both loves him limitlessly and wants him to show the same extravagant love to all the human family. This is what revelation is about; this is his agenda, the task given to him. How it is to be achieved is not set out beforehand. It requires a consistent responding to the demands of wisdom and love in the emerging circumstances of life.

The consequences of his choices and discernments bring him to the Passion. At this point occurs the final choice of his life. Instead of trying to escape or to endure his death in bitter resentment and hatred, he chooses to accept the cross in self-sacrificing love for the good of us all. Thus, he reveals the existence of a love that embraces all the evil of the world. This is the love that is given to me, and it is intended for extravagant sharing. It is not for myself alone.

Choosing Well

Ignatian spirituality focuses on the making of good decisions. What Ignatius would want for us is "discerning love"—that is, all our decisions should flow from a wise love. Solomon in the Old Testament asked for a "discerning heart," and so can we.

This discerning, or well-thought-out, love, is not easy to come by. But with practice it becomes more spontaneously the pattern of our lives, so that while remaining our very *human* selves we can live out a life of close intimacy with the *divine* persons. This is what Christian living is meant to be about. On the surface, such a life may seem to be very ordinary, but there is nothing ordinary about it at all! It is a remarkable thing to come across people who make statements like these:

> *"I do the best I can. I try to put God and other people first."*
>
> *"I often don't know what to do. So I turn to God and sometimes read a bit of the Gospels, and then things get clearer."*
>
> *"There were lots of things in my life that I would have wanted different. But they were the way they were, and all I could do was put up with them patiently and with as much love as I could dredge up."*

Jesus could have made these very statements. His life has no fixed pattern. He is the one who is pre-eminently led by the Spirit, and the Spirit which "blows where it will" leads him into an extraordinary variety of situations. The one constant in his life is that he puts the Father and the Father's plans for the world first. We are invited to do the same. But we are free. The Good News is all about love and freedom. However, when you put these together, there emerges **a responsibility for others, born of love**. God entrusts us to one another. My neighbours are God's friends, God's beloveds, so they must be mine also! It is love of this sort that keeps the world from sliding into total chaos.

God Among Us

The God of Ignatian spirituality is not only the God of the tabernacle, the sanctuary, or the cloister, but is God among us, God of the everyday, of the ordinary, of the marketplace and the Stock Exchange. In becoming human, God "moves house" and becomes God-with-us. In Jesus, God is with his people; he is as vulnerable and unsafe as they are. Paul is told as he goes to persecute the Damascus Christians, "I am Jesus and you are persecuting ME." He takes very personally how we treat our needy neighbour: "You're doing that to ME!" God is close.

Ignatian spirituality does not float above our messy world but is earthed among people, wherever and however they may be. It embraces the poor. It stands with the marginalised and the victims of our world. It expresses a faith that seeks to do justice. It animates us to work for human development because God desires dignity for all people. Where our instinct is to bypass the poor, the drop-outs, the wrecks of humanity, Ignatian spirituality challenges us with the simple but shattering truth that *everyone is to be loved*.

Because it is sympathetic to the human condition, Ignatian spirituality is flexible in regard to structures and institutions. These are necessary because we are social beings, but they are not ends in themselves. They are to be adapted and transformed continuously so that they may truly serve the good of the people. This includes the Church, which, as the Second Vatican Council says, is *always in need of reform*.

Keeping God in View

Ignatius did not lay down rules about the length of our prayers. Instead he advised that to keep going in the way God wishes, we should keep God always before our eyes. We are to touch base with God in everything we intend to do. This will involve

- time spent alone with God in order to be won over to God's values and attitudes, as shown dramatically in the life of Jesus.
- time for reflection with Jesus on how the day went; planning with him the decisions to be made for the next day.
- times for sharing with others. Salvation is not private but a group event. Hence the importance of the prayer group, the parish, the Eucharist; we survive by solidarity.

- A developing openness to God's presence everywhere—in nature, in people, in beauty, in the good things that come our way. But also in the challenging situations. Here Ignatius would have us ask: "What ought I do to help people here?"

In this perspective, life and prayer merge. When we undertake an activity out of belief that God wishes it of us, this is *living prayer,* prayer in action. Life no longer has two parts. My ordinary life and my life with God become unified.

Ignatian spirituality recognises too how easily we can be misled. We can be motivated subtly by our own needs rather than the needs of others. The Ignatian Review of Consciousness comes in here. It is not an introverted exercise but a time for noticing the moods of consolation and desolation that play upon our spirits. It uncovers our blind spots and shadows and enables us to see where the movements of our hearts are taking us. Spiritual guidance can help us interpret what is going on.

A Beautiful Risk

It was Plato who said that life is a risk, but a beautiful risk. To live a life in God's companionship is certainly to embrace a life of risk. Ignatian spirituality carries a health warning! But it encourages a person to begin a journey into the freedom and joy which is the very life of God.

It invites you to seek and find and seek again. It emphasises the divine dimension hidden in your human experiences. In your mistakes and failures you can learn how to proceed better the next time. You find yourself in the company of the God of Surprises. Together with God, you plan what to do next. You neither drift through life in a bored way, nor are you dragged violently into something for which you have no desire. Rather, you find harmony, the harmony of two sets of desires, divine and human. God and yourself focus on one common concern: the gathering of all humankind into the final community of love. Life then becomes a great and exciting adventure. Happy hunting!

Note: There are many websites that will open up Ignatian spirituality for you, such as www.sacredspace.ie; Creighton University—https://onlineministries.creighton.edu/CollaborativeMinistry/cmo-retreat.html; and www.ignatianspirituality.com.

Acknowledgments

My thanks to all who have helped me over the years in my search for God; to Maura Lynch; Sr. Anne Lyons, PBVM; and Colette McCarthy, who read the manuscript through and contributed valuable insights.

Thanks to the staff of Messenger Publications for their expertise and patience in guiding the book into the light of day.

About the Author

Dr. Brian Grogan, SJ, is a former President of Milltown Institute of Theology and Philosophy, Dublin, and is Emeritus Associate Professor of Spirituality there. He also served as director and editor of Sacred Space, the international prayer web site of the Irish Jesuits. He has written extensively on Ignatian spirituality and has lectured and led workshops for many years. Currently he is Superior of the Jesuit House of Writers in Dublin.

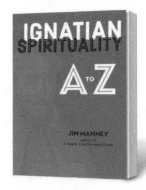

MORE BOOKS ABOUT **IGNATIAN SPIRITUALITY**

Experiencing God in the Ordinary

WILLIAM A. BARRY, SJ

We tend to look for God in dramatic or miraculous moments, but such expectations can blind us to God's ongoing presence. What if God is already with us, in this very moment?

Whether we are in pain or crisis or are simply wondering why God would be in the mundane details of our lives, *Experiencing God in the Ordinary* can nurture our hope—that God is always present and can be found in an ordinary day. This book is perfect for devotional reading, retreat, or small-group discussion.

Paperback | 978-0-8294-5033-0 | $14.95

Finding God in the Mess
Meditations for Mindful Living

JIM DEEDS (Photographs by Brendan McManus, SJ)

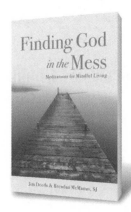

Our busy modern lives distract us and cause us stress. Technology, media, jobs, family, appointments, hobbies—it can all feel like a mess. How do we carve out time for mindful contemplation and prayer?

Finding God in the Mess features meditations and pages to write down our thoughts, making it the perfect tool to help us learn to pause, to take time to be with God, to contemplate our lives, and to recognize God's presence in all of it, especially the hard times.

Paperback | 978-0-8294-4910-5 | $12.95

What's Your Decision?

How to Make Choices with Confidence and Clarity: An Ignatian Approach to Decision Making

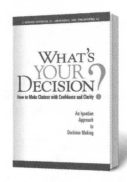

J. MICHAEL SPAROUGH, SJ; TIM HIPSKIND, SJ; and JIM MANNEY

What's Your Decision? is a fast-moving, personal, and highly practical book. In this book, the authors introduce readers to the time-tested Ignatian approach to effective decision making.

Based on the insights of St. Ignatius, this book helps us understand that a God decision always precedes a good decision: When we invite God into the decision-making process, we find the freedom to make the best choice.

Paperback I 978-0-8294-3148-3 I $10.95

God's Voice Within

The Ignatian Way to Discover God's Will

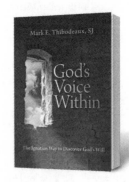

MARK E. THIBODEAUX, SJ

God's Voice Within is intended for people who know that there is more to the spiritual life than they are currently experiencing and are ready to take the next step in their walk of faith by making effective discernment—specifically Ignatian discernment—a daily practice.

Ultimately, *God's Voice Within* teaches us to discern what is at the root of our actions and emotions, which in turn allows us to respond to God's promptings inside us rather than unconsciously reacting to life around us.

Paperback I 978-0-8294-2861-2 I $14.95

A Simple, Life-Changing Prayer
Discovering the Power of St. Ignatius Loyola's Examen

JIM MANNEY

In *A Simple, Life-Changing Prayer*, Jim Manney introduces Christians to a 500-year-old form of prayer—the Examen. St. Ignatius Loyola developed the Examen for the purpose of nurturing a reflective habit of mind constantly attuned to God's presence.

By following five simple yet powerful steps for praying the Examen, we can encounter the God whose presence in our lives can make all the difference in the world.

English: Paperback I 978-0-8294-3535-1 I $9.95
Spanish: Paperback I 978-0-8294-4389-9 I $9.95

Reimagining the Ignatian Examen
Fresh Ways to Pray from Your Day

MARK E. THIBODEAUX, SJ

Join Father Thibodeaux as he guides you through new and unique versions of the Examen, totally flexible and adaptable to your life. In ten minutes, you can tailor your daily prayer practice to fit your personal and situational needs, further enhancing and deepening your meditation.

Reimagining the Ignatian Examen will lead you through a fresh and stimulating reflection on your past day, your present state of being, and your spiritual desires and needs for tomorrow.

English: Paperback I 978-0-8294-4244-1 I $12.95
Spanish: Paperback I 978-0-8294-4512-1 I $12.95

Also available as a free app for download on iOS and Android.

TO ORDER: Call **800.621.1008**, visit **store.loyolapress.com**, or visit your local bookseller.